WELLNESS IN THE WORKPLACE

How to Plan, Implement and Evaluate a Wellness Program

Merlene T. Sherman

From the Library of
THE PERFORMANCE GROUP
10627 - 124 Street
Edmonton, AB T5N 1S5
(780) 414-1234

From the resource library of :
The Performance Group
10123-123 St.
Edmonton, AB
(403) 414-1234

CRISP PUBLICATIONS, INC.
Los Altos, California

WELLNESS IN THE WORKPLACE
How to Plan, Implement and Evaluate a Wellness Program

Merlene T. Sherman

CREDITS
Editor: **Anne Knight**
Designer: **Carol Harris**
Typesetting: **Interface Studio**
Cover Design: **Carol Harris**
Artwork: **Ralph Mapson**

All rights reserved. No part of this book may be reproduced or transmitted in any form or by any means now known or to be invented, electronic or mechanical, including photocopying, recording, or by any information storage or retrieval system without written permission from the author or publisher, except for the brief inclusion of quotations in a review.

Copyright © 1990 by Crisp Publications, Inc.
Printed in the United States of America

English language Crisp books are distributed worldwide. Our major international distributors include:

CANADA: Reid Publishing Ltd., Box 69559—109 Thomas St., Oakville, Ontario Canada L6J 7R4. TEL: (416) 842-4428, FAX: (416) 842-9327

AUSTRALIA: Career Builders, P. O. Box 1051, Springwood, Brisbane, Queensland, Australia 4127. TEL: 841-1061, FAX: 841-1580

NEW ZEALAND: Career Builders, P. O. Box 571, Manurewa, Auckland, New Zealand. TEL: 266-5276, FAX: 266-4152

JAPAN: Phoenix Associates Co., Mizuho Bldg. 2-12-2, Kami Osaki, Shinagawa-Ku, Tokyo 141, Japan. TEL: 3-443-7231, FAX: 3-443-7640

Selected Crisp titles are also available in other languages. Contact International Rights Manager Tim Polk at (415) 949-4888 for more information.

Library of Congress Catalog Card Number 89-81245
Sherman, Merlene T.
Wellness In The Workplace
ISBN 1-56052-020-5

INTRODUCTION

This is a book your company can't afford to be without. It's a treasury of health promotion ideas written for CEO's, managers, supervisors, health personnel, department heads, education directors, health and safety committees, and anyone else who is interested in worksite wellness.

Written in a direct, no-nonsense style with an occasional twist of humor, it shows you how to develop and maintain wellness programs with practical, low-cost techniques, and provides enlightening examples of thriving wellness programs across the country. You'll find hundreds of creative ideas to enhance existing programs, plus a host of innovative strategies to help revitalize wellness programs that have lost their zip.

Whether companies are small or large, whether they have only two employees or thousands, they can use this book as a guide to help employees enjoy improving their health. Lower costs, better morale, and increased production are just a few of the exciting ways that your company will benefit by being involved in a wellness program. But more importantly, when you participate in health promotion, you are taking care of your most valuable resource: your employees.

Merlene T. Sherman

MERLENE T. SHERMAN

CONTENTS

SECTION 1

THE WHYS OF WORKPLACE WELLNESS

RUNAWAY HEALTH COSTS

RUNAWAY HEALTH COSTS

Dateline: Houston, Texas. City officials reported today that Houston closed down last year. Not one of its nearly two million residents went to work during the entire year. The city was not on official holiday; all its residents were just too ill or disabled to report to work.

This news item sounds unbelievable, but it represents the number of employee work days American businesses lost last year due to illness and disability. According to government statistics, 500 million workdays per year, or enough to close down a city the size of Houston for a full 365 days, were lost because of ill health, at a cost of billions of dollars.

In addition, the health insurance industry reports that employee and employer premiums have increased by the alarming rate of 15-30 percent over the past few years. Some economists estimate the average health bill for a workplace will soon equal a company's after-tax yearly profits!

How would you like to compete against these financial health care odds? "For me, healthcare costs are $700 a car and still going up at twice the rate of inflation," says Chrysler Corporation Chairman Lee Iacocca.

The costs do not end with your bill for health care. Poor health in the workplace can result in chaos. Think of the customers you could lose if your switchboard operator were sick and telephone calls weren't put through. Thousands of dollars can be lost if communications break down.

Imagine the havoc created if your top negotiator becomes disabled the day before labor talks are scheduled to begin. Frustration levels skyrocket and morale plummets.

The staggering consequences of illness and disability have forced companies to respond aggressively with campaigns to prevent sickness and injury. Health care in the office, at the factory, or on the job site is no longer satisfied by an annual check-up and a tidy health insurance package.

CHRONIC DISEASE REARS ITS HEAD

Until recently, most people in the U.S. didn't take responsibility for their own health. For years, physicians and the public health system assured us not to worry, that the best medical resources were at our disposal. Most childhood diseases had been wiped out by the miracle of immunization, but if a person did get sick, we were assured that medical technology and hospitals could fix most anything. In short, there seemed to be no compelling reason for people to be concerned about preventive health.

Those who were conscientious about their health tried to find a physician who could cure their ills and keep them healthy. Comedian Henny Youngman alluded to the insistence upon finding a good doctor with his story about the man who was seriously ill and went to the finest medical specialist in the country. After the examination, the physician presented the man with a bill for $500.

"I can't pay this, Doc. I haven't got two nickels to my name."

"If you haven't got any money," the doctor says, "why did you come to the finest specialist in the country?"

"Listen," the patient replied, "when it comes to my health, money is no object."

By the middle of the twentieth century, acute infectious diseases were largely under control, but chronic disease had become a major threat. Immunizations could not prevent cancer, heart disease, or stroke. Americans were shocked to learn that in many instances unhealthy lifestyles caused chronic illnesses. Too much alcohol is associated with cirrhosis of the liver, smoking with cancer, and poor nutrition and inactivity with cardiovascular disease.

The most up-to-date health data made it clear that responsibility for lifestyle choices and health rests squarely on our own shoulders.

LIFESTYLE CHOICES

People who are healthy:

- enjoy life more
- communicate better
- have more stamina
- have better coping skills
- have a greater commitment to work
- are more enthusiastic and productive
- have a more positive outlook on life

We can't control the heredity and age factors in our lives, but lifestyle choices *are* controllable and offer our best chance at wellness. Health professionals term poor behavior choices ''risk factors.'' The higher the number of risk factors, the more likely the possibility of disease and premature death.

This is where worksite wellness programs have an important part to play.

HEALTHY PEOPLE DON'T DO THIS

WORKSITE WELLNESS

Today, most companies are stepping up their efforts to enhance the lives and improve the health of their workers. A new dimension to staying healthy is added when companies plan wellness programs (also called health promotion programs) to help employees achieve and maintain good physical and mental health.

For every $9 that a company pays to an employee, it spends a substantial $1 on health care. Control Data Corporation's four-year study of 15,000 employees showed that workers with the worst life-style habits ran up the biggest medical bills. Health care costs for obese people were 11 percent higher than those for thin ones. And workers who routinely failed to buckle up spent 54 percent more days in the hospital than those who used seat belts.

Health promotion programs emphasize a ''wellness concept'' that encourages adopting a lifestyle aimed at achieving and maintaining physical, mental, and spiritual well-being at home and on the job. Wellness is good business. What's good for the employee is good for the employer.

COMPANY BENEFITS

The principal goal of workplace health promotion programs is healthier employees. But companies also reap benefits through lower health insurance premiums, reduced absenteeism and turnover, increased performance and productivity, improved employee morale, and enhanced company image. Take a look at the way a wellness program can pay off for you.

LOWER HEALTH INSURANCE PREMIUMS

More and more companies are self-insuring their health costs these days. They pay claims out of their own budget and select insurance companies to administer and process employee claims. If your company is self-insured or insured at an experience-based rate, reduced use of health services lowers the cost of insurance premiums.

Researchers estimate that premiums for group coverage costs can rise or fall a significant 20 percent based on employee lifestyles alone. The effect on individual insurance rates is even greater.

Specific Insurance Reductions

In an attempt to reduce health care claims and insurance premiums, some companies schedule medical self-care classes to teach their employees how to self-administer certain tests, treatments, and therapies. And even though employees are taught when to call the doctor, they are inclined to seek professional care less often, because they are more confident about their health.

John Hancock Financial Services in Boston goes all out to lower premiums and reduce medical costs associated with respiratory problems. The company's health promotion programs include quit-smoking workshops, the John Hancock Former Smokers Network, and the autumn observance of the American Cancer Society's Great American Smokeout.

Reduced use of medical services pays off in a big way for the city employees in Bellvue, Washington. When the company pays fewer health claims, a portion of the money saved is given to employees who observe good health practices. It's a "win-win" situation for the workers and the city.

REDUCED WORKERS' COMPENSATION COSTS

Fitness classes for employees do wonders to increase body strength and promote agility, stamina, and flexibility. The more fit your employees, the fewer number of workers' compensation claims you'll have to pay. Unless, of course, you have an Erma Bombeck in your midst who maintains that the only reason to take up jogging is "to hear heavy breathing again...."

My Aching Back

Back injuries account for 80 percent of workers' compensation costs for some companies. Annual costs to employers are 93 million lost work days, $5 billion in medical expenses, and an incredible $12 billion in legal and insurance costs. Burlington Industries is one of many innovative companies across the country that has started "Healthy Back Programs" to prevent back injuries and reduce workers' compensation claims.

Employee Assistance Programs (often a part of health promotion programs) also lower workers' compensation costs. Within one year after General Motors started an Employee Assistance Program, sickness and accident benefit payments were decreased by an amazing 60 percent.

LESS EMPLOYEE ABSENTEEISM

Age, race, gender, education, and marital status are not predictors of how faithfully an employee will come to work. There is, however, a strong connection between physical activity and good attendance. A recent report issued by the U.S. Chamber of Commerce indicated that physically fit employees are less likely to miss work than their out-of-shape colleagues.

King-Size Savings

Canada Life Assurance Company reported a hefty 42 percent reduction in absenteeism among those involved in the company's health and fitness program. This resulted in an average reduction of 2.5 employee work days lost each year. Other studies have shown up to 55 percent reduction in absenteeism for workplace fitness participants. Talk about savings!

There's more. When employees perceive that you have a sincere concern for their well-being, their increased loyalty and sense of responsibility to the company become by-products of your efforts.

DECREASED TURNOVER

Picture this. A clerical worker, a mid-level manager, and a top executive will stop working next month due to ill health and death. Your assignment is to estimate the monetary loss of these people to your company.

The shocking facts are that it can cost your company up to $4000 to replace the clerical worker, up to $8500 for the manager, and a mind-boggling 1.5 million to replace the executive. Is it any wonder that companies are looking to wellness programs to help their employees become healthier?

Staying Power

We all know that poor health is not the only reason for job turnover. Employees are more likely to remain on the job when they are satisfied with their companies. Often times, a wellness program is the extra perk that creates the satisfaction and staying power for employees.

You will have fewer job openings and lower recruitment costs if your employees are satisfied with their work situations and healthy enough to work everyday. They also won't be out on the streets looking for other jobs.

IT IS EXPENSIVE TO REPLACE PEOPLE

INCREASED PERFORMANCE AND PRODUCTIVITY

A Case Study

Sue Terrell writes government proposals for the Miller Agency. After working four years at her job, she began having back problems. Agonizing pain made it so difficult for her to concentrate on writing that her performance quickly deteriorated.

After medical tests indicated Sue needed to strengthen her back muscles, she decided she needed an incentive to walk on a regular basis. So she joined the walking club at work. Bingo! Within two months Sue's back was stronger, and it was easier for her to write creatively again. She had turned her life around with a healthier lifestyle and was benefiting from a pain-free back and new ''walking friends.'' What's more, the Miller Agency retained a valued employee who was again able to achieve high performance and productivity.

Employees who participate in wellness programs can relieve physical and emotional problems and do a better job. But to benefit, they must be *active* participants. Sue's return to productivity would not have occured without her decision to strengthen her back muscles by joining the walking club.

The more your employees participate in wellness programs, the healthier and more productive they will be. NASA reports that employees who participate in their fitness program show a 52 percent improvement in job performance. Plan your own study. You're sure to discover an encouraging correlation between employee wellness participation and productivity.

HIGHER EMPLOYEE MORALE

WARNING TO ALL EMPLOYEES
FIRINGS WILL CONTINUE UNTIL MORALE IMPROVES

Companies that promote employee health have little need for such absurb, tongue-in-cheek notices. When employees participate in wellness programs, concern for their good health is likely to catapult them to greater job satisfaction and improved morale.

"M'm! M'm! Good!"

A study at Campbell Soup Company showed that the positive attitude created by their health and fitness program even rubs off on employees who do not participate. Employees who were not wellness participants say that health and fitness center staff would still take the time to express concern over their fitness needs. One employee noted that even if the health and fitness activities were located in a dungeon, they would continue to have an uplifting affect on the company's morale.

With results like these, what are you waiting for?

IMPROVED COMPANY IMAGE

Everyone wants to feel good, so it's easy to understand why people are attracted to wellness programs. When prospective employees are interviewing for jobs, wellness programs can be an enticing benefit. Health and fitness programs have drawing power to attract more applicants.

You can't beat the image created by a well-run health promotion program. Healthy employees are all the publicity you need to cast the company in a leadership role in the community.

POSITIVE IMAGE AND THEN SOME

One midwestern company that has successfully created a positive image with their wellness program is Scherer Brothers Lumber Company in Minneapolis, Minnesota.

''Everything that's good for people is in one of our programs,'' boasts owner Greg Scherer.

Employees can snack on apples, oranges, bananas, and in-season fruits provided free by the company. Nutritious midday meals are served without charge to all employees, and an exercise program is available to any employee who wants to participate. There's ''well pay'' but no ''sick leave,'' and the only excused absences from work are vacation, holidays, funerals, or jury duty.

A progressive company that looks toward wellness education is a healthy company.

''Cure people's ills and you make them healthy for a day. Teach them to stay well and you make them healthy for a lifetime.''

With a company philosophy like that, who could find a better place to work?

''TODAY'S SPECIALS INCLUDE OAT BRAN, CARROTS AND APPLES.''

HALE AND HEARTY PROGRAMS

Worksite wellness has taken hold and promises to play a vital role in companies for years to come. More and more companies in the United States have successfully started health promotion programs that continue to pay dividends. Three creative examples will show you why.

Safeway

It's called "Buns on the Run" and it was designed by Safeway in Clackamas, Oregon, to reduce a rising number of accidents, injuries, and cases of muscle fatigue related to work performed in the retail food industry.

Professionals from the university, a nearby hospital, and the director of the Governor's Council on Sports, Health, and Fitness helped two managers start Safeway's all-volunteer program. Aerobic fitness classes are offered five days a week, and guest speakers discuss injuries, nutrition, weight control, sports medicine, smoking cessation, and stress management. There's a fitness room furnished with exercise equipment and a quarter-mile running track located behind the Safeway bread plant.

Preliminary results after 21 months in operation revealed smoking cessation, increased flexibility, employee weight loss, and reductions in pulse and blood pressure. Other improvements included changes in lifestyle for entire families and unexpected strengthening of family bonds. A real plus!

Johnson and Johnson

When Johnson and Johnson decided to go all out to control increasing illness and accident costs, they started their Live for Life program by offering their employees the opportunity to be "the healthiest in the world." Health screenings and activities involving fitness, nutrition, weight control, stress management, smoking cessation, and blood pressure intervention soon became a standard part of the program.

Since Live for Life began, health costs have been cut by a phenomenal 34 percent for participating workers. A five-year study showed annual inpatient costs were $33 and $34 less for participating employees who needed to be hospitalized. And as you would expect, participants also had fewer hospital admissions and days in the hospital.

Tenneco

After Jim Ketelson, chairman and Tenneco CEO, underwent by-pass heart surgery, he decided that the workplace could provide employees with an opportunity to take better care of themselves. Thus, the beginning of Tenneco's wellness program.

Their health and fitness center provides supervised exercise and cardiovascular fitness programs. Among the many classes offered are CPR, women's health, prenatal education, and defensive driving. There's even a special dining facility for calorie and nutrition-conscious employees.

The good news is that health care claims for Tenneco's participating employees have been reduced by 55 percent for men and 44 percent for women. Jim Kettelson's idea more than pays off.

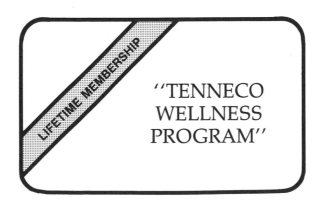

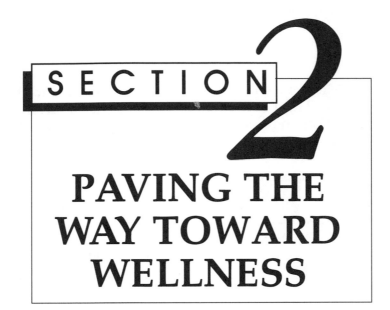

SECTION 2

PAVING THE WAY TOWARD WELLNESS

STARTING OR EXPANDING A PROGRAM

WELLNESS PROGRAMS AT WORK

You won't find a better setting for a wellness program than the worksite. People spend a large portion of their day at work, and the needed structure for programs is already in place. Work and health are both extremely important to employees, so it makes sense to meld the two together.

Consider these five significant questions when developing or expanding a health promotion program:

1. Are your employee needs a top priority?
2. What are your company's wellness needs?
3. What are your company's health promotion capabilities?
4. What are your community's health promotion capabilities?
5. What are the goals of your wellness program?

EMPLOYEES' NEEDS

The best-laid plans won't get off the ground if your major goal of wellness is only to cut company costs. The primary goal of health programs must be to positively affect its participants. Employees need to participate and personally gain from programs to support them.

Information Collection

Take the guesswork out of determining employee needs and interests by gathering the following information:
- age
- sex
- education
- type of work performed
- ethnic background
- what employees want
- employee health problems
- seasonal aspects of the job
- geographical aspects of the job

If you collect information from employees or the company nurse pinpoints a high incidence of back problems, that's your clue to plan a program in back care. Are there employees who say they want help with a diet? Since everybody knows weight-reduction is not just ''wishful shrinking,'' a well-planned diet class will be met with enthusiasm.

COMPANY NEEDS

Delve into the needs of the company before beginning or expanding a wellness program. Take a minute to rate the results that your company wants from a wellness program. (1. Immediate priority, 2. Future consideration, 3. Not needed)

- ☐ less turnover
- ☐ fewer accidents
- ☐ less absenteeism
- ☐ better performance
- ☐ healthier employees
- ☐ increased productivity
- ☐ improved company image

- ☐ improved employee morale
- ☐ reduced health insurance premiums
- ☐ reduced workers' compensation claims
- ☐ _____
- ☐ _____
- ☐ _____
- ☐ _____

Set realistic time frames for meeting your needs. If your company wants quick results, plan hypertension screening and accident prevention programs. Nutrition and weight reduction programs take longer to show results.

The bottom line is that wellness programs must be helpful to employees *and* cost-effective for the company. A safety program can only be justified if it keeps employees safe, reduces the accident rate, and benefits the company with fewer associated costs.

Industry Survey

After you have examined the needs of your company, go one step further and do an industry analysis by responding with a YES or NO to these four questions.

YES	NO	
_____	_____	Do you know about similar companies in the country that have health promotion programs? Would some of their ideas help your employees?
_____	_____	Are there local businesses with wellness programs from which you could get more information?
_____	_____	Is there a wellness council in the area that could help?
_____	_____	Can you combine ideas and programs with other companies that have similar goals?

WELLNESS PROGRAMS (Continued)

COMPANY CAPABILITIES

It's easy to determine if your company has the capabilities to start a wellness program. Just use this handy reference list and put a check ☑ to indicate your resources as adequate or inadequate.

Company resouces	Adequate	Inadequate
Labor support	———————	———————
Management support	———————	———————
Appropriate timing	———————	———————
Space and equipment	———————	———————
Enthusiastic employees	———————	———————
Available program staff	———————	———————
Money to start and maintain a wellness program	———————	———————

Programs can vary from no-cost to low-cost to expensive, but only a few firms have large facilities and staffs to support extensive health promotion agendas. The amount of space available also determines the types of programs and equipment you can have.

The people-issue weighs heavily in start-up or expansion of wellness programs. Are management and labor (if you have unions) fully committed to wellness programs? Are employees enthusiastic about participating? Look at the availability of your staff and the way you'd invite them to assist with the programs.

You may be involved in health promotion without knowing it. If a juice bar has already been added to your employee lounge, you have taken a step toward wellness programming. Has the company reduced noise levels in work spaces or established a smoke free work environment? Then you're well on the way to health promotion programming. The expansion of activities should be easy.

Don't be discouraged if previous wellness programs were not successful at your company. That was then; this is NOW. This time employees may respond more positively and managers may be more supportive of programs. After all, those past workshops on ''Creative Suffering'' and ''Overcoming Peace of Mind'' may not have been just the right thing to strike the fancy of your employees at the time.

Whether your commitment involves one health seminar or a series of elaborate efforts, the message to employees is the same. You care about their well-being.

COMMUNITY CAPABILITIES

When you don't have the time, staff, skills, or information available in your company for wellness programming, check out your community for help. Superb resources might be right at your fingertips. There are two types of community support systems.

Type 1. Universities, colleges, and hospitals have an abundance of professionals who are often available to give assistance.

Type 2. Private companies, volunteer agencies, and non-profit organizations that are in business to provide health promotion services are a gold mine of resources.

Don't overlook other wellness programs in your community. If the local YMCA is sponsoring exercise sessions for adults, consider encouraging your employees to attend the Y instead of duplicating their efforts at your workplace.

GOAL SETTING

Decision-making will be as difficult as nailing Jello to a tree if you don't set goals to determine the health programs that you want. Place an (X) by the goals that are suitable for your company and add others of your own.

Goals

_____ To reduce turnover
_____ To cut health costs
_____ To reduce absenteeism
_____ To improve company image
_____ To improve employee morale
_____ To establish a healthy environment
_____ To improve performance and productivity
_____ To help employees change unhealthy lifestyles
_____ (List your own goals) _____
_____ _____
_____ _____

A survey of 31 small companies across the nation indicated that goals to contain costs ranked a distant second to increased morale, reduced absenteeism, and other human relations considerations. These employers were more interested in goals improving quality of worklife than in lowering costs.

ESTABLISHING OBJECTIVES

Once you have set goals, are you ready to establish objectives that can be easily measured and evaluated? Take a look at these compelling examples. They'll inspire you to create some dynamic objectives of your own.

OBJECTIVE	RECOMMENDED ACTION
To have a large number of employees take part in health promotion programs.	Schedule nutrition classes that have wide appeal and are useful to everyone.
To have the community take notice of our company and its programs.	Plan high visibility health fairs or cholesterol screening for employees and the public.
(List your own)	(List your own)
_____	_____
_____	_____

IF IT ISN'T WRITTEN, IT ISN'T A GOAL

MANAGEMENT ISSUES

LEADERSHIP

Prelude to a disaster:

- The Vice President of Human Relations asks all employees to attend an afternoon seminar on stress management.
- The Office Manager does not want the office staff to attend the seminar because they won't be able to finish the mailing that has been assigned.

Obviously, the people in this management situation need to put their heads together. Mixed signals and lack of support can quickly sabotage the best of wellness programs. To be successful, health promotion programs must be an organizational priority for top and middle management. Support that comes from top management can be active or passive. But nothing sells a program more effectively than a CEO who actively supports the program by participating in the wellness walk or volunteering to help with blood pressure screenings at the health fair.

To help get the ball rolling and guarantee a successful operation with new programs, you can hire an outside consultant or organize a committee or leadership team with wide-spread representation of employees. And that's not all. You will ultimately need a director to make sure that things happen. Often, the director works in the education, personnel, human resources, or medical department.

If your committee members and the wellness director are the movers and shakers in the organization, their energy is sure to carry over into exciting health promotion efforts. For more extensive programs, a wellness director and staff can be hired.

PROGRAM LENGTH

Experiment with sessions of different lengths to find the best times for your employees. The number of times you schedule a program and the length of sessions can make a big difference in employee attendance.

- Single-session programs are often too short to help employees resolve health concerns.
- Programs extended over long periods may discourage attendance if an employee has to miss more than one session.

Conoco, Inc. in Houston, Texas, has spectacular success in securing good attendance by offering wellness programs in four or five-week sessions with a break in between. After a one-week break, employees are asked to sign up for the next group of classes. If workers have missed several sessions, the sign-up gives them a chance to re-register and start over.

EMPLOYEE OR COMPANY TIME

Will your employees be improving their health on company time or on their own time? Be sure to resolve this critical issue during the early stages of planning.

1. You can schedule programs before work, after work, or during the lunch hour and expect employees to participate in wellness activities on their own time.
2. You can provide screening and educational programs during work hours and allow employees time off to attend activities.

Scheduling health programs for non-work hours could only convey the idea that wellness is not a priority with management. Some companies compromise with a split-time arrangement by scheduling activities early or late in the day. Employees are given 30 minutes of work time (4:00-4:30 p.m.) to attend 60-minute health sessions, and they are expected to spend 30 minutes of personal time to complete the session (4:30-5:00 p.m.). This solution works amazingly well for many employers and employees.

CONFIDENTIALITY

Your assurance of total privacy will make employees a lot more willing to participate in worksite health promotion. Health is a very personal matter, and employees have to know that their health problems will not be revealed or jeopardize their jobs. If an employee has AIDS, will the information remain confidential?

Among the most crucial elements in assuring program success is maintaining confidentiality. The following guidelines should ensure that it is.

1. Establish confidentiality policies and procedures.
2. Make sure health data is stored in a secure area.
3. Make sure that employees know that management follows specific confidentiality guidelines.
4. Offer an orientation session on confidentiality issues for the people responsible for conducting physicals, reviewing health risk appraisals, and handling employee health information.

CONFIDENTIALITY STARTS WITH THE INDIVIDUAL

EMPLOYEE INVOLVEMENT

You'll discover how easy it is to develop or expand a wellness program if you involve employees at all levels in the planning process. Here's how to do it.

Brainstorm	You'll be surprised at the dynamite ideas employees have when they can make their needs known to you.
Hold informal meetings	Involvement increases the control, ownership, and responsibility employees feel when they can actively participate in the planning process.
Work with group spokespersons	Tap the energy and ideas of small employee groups by gaining support from employees who are their spokespersons.
Solicit help	Draw on the talents of your employees and ask them to teach some courses. It's an eye-opener to learn who is qualified to teach classes in CPR or aerobic dancing.
Request evaluation	Ask employees to evaluate programs. Involvement stimulates interest and creates positive feelings about the company.
Survey employee interests and concerns	Design your own survey or use the one on the facing page as a quick means to discover employee interests.

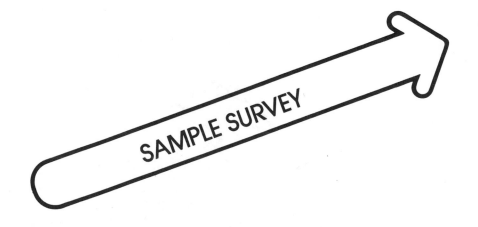

EMPLOYEE WELLNESS SURVEY

Please take a few moments to fill out. From the following list of activities and programs, check the ones you would be most interested in and would attend.

Interested **Will Attend**

Interested	Will Attend	
_____	_____	1. Alcohol and Drug Abuse Control
_____	_____	2. Assertiveness Training
_____	_____	3. Cancer Risk Reduction
_____	_____	4. Cardiopulmonary Resuscitation (CPR)
_____	_____	5. Positive Thinking
_____	_____	6. Dental Disease Prevention
_____	_____	7. First Aid
_____	_____	8. Health Awareness Program
_____	_____	9. Glaucoma Screening
_____	_____	10. Goal Achievement
_____	_____	11. Healthy Back
_____	_____	12. Heart Attack Risk Reduction
_____	_____	13. Hypertension Control
_____	_____	14. Nutrition
_____	_____	15. Physical Fitness Activities
_____	_____	16. Safety-Accident Prevention
_____	_____	17. Stress Management
_____	_____	18. Weight Management
_____	_____	19. Physical Fitness Lectures
_____	_____	20. Other _____

2. Would you attend one or more of the above programs if they were offered at a convenient time? ____Yes ____No ____Maybe
   What time is most convenient for you? _____

3. Do you have a planned, regular program of exercise (swimming, walking, jogging, exercise machines) in which you participate at least three times a week? ____Yes ____No

4. Would you like to participate in an exercise/fitness program that was geared to your level of fitness? ____Yes ____No

5. What activities would you like to learn? _____

6. What types of exercise programs would you like to see at the worksite?
   ____Aerobic ____Jazzercise ____Calisthenics ____Other _____

7. Would your spouse and/or family participate in a health promotion program at your worksite if they were invited? ____Yes ____No

8. If one or more of the programs or activities listed above that you selected as the most interesting to attend were offered at a convenient time, and at a reasonable cost, would you probably attend that program? ____Yes ____No

9. Would you feel comfortable participating in a program with your co-workers? ____Yes ____No

10. In the space below, write any other health care or health promotion ideas or concerns that may have been triggered by the previous questions.

   What hours do you work? ____a.m./p.m. to ____a.m./p.m.
   Are you ____Male or ____Female?
   What age group are you in? ____20-30 ____31-40 ____41-50 ____Over 50
   Are you: ____Administrative or ____Shop?

Reprinted with permission from Valmont Industries, Inc., Valley, Nebraska.

DIVERSE PROGRAM MODELS

To give you a sense of the diversity of wellness programs, let's take a look at programs functioning at different levels.

AWARENESS PROGRAMS

Informal Encouragement

- Sometimes, health promotion programs are not formally organized. Employees are simply encouraged by the company to adopt healthy lifestyle habits or become involved in physical fitness programs.
- Spreading the word about health through newsletters, paycheck inserts, and bulletin boards is a favorite way companies make employees aware of wellness with low-cost efforts.
- Some companies pay employee memberships to local YMCA's, health clubs, schools, or recreation centers.

Hawaii's Chevron Refinery

When Chevron Refinery in Honolulu started a blockbuster refinery-wide safety awareness program, on-and-off-the-job injuries plummeted. Throughout the refinery there are reminders to use safety measures.

The company promotes safety awareness through awards, slogans, posters, contests, bulletin boards, home mailings, and even a billboard. There's a safety meeting every month, publication of accident statistics, and a safety council to measure the level of safety awareness.

Arkansas' Atlantic Research

Even low-cost flyers can make a positive difference. Atlantic Research Corporation in Camden, Arkansas makes their 530 employees aware of wellness with health flyers that are placed in break rooms throughout the plant. If workers don't get health hints during breaks, they can attend education sessions that focus on a different health topic each month.

SPECIFIC PROGRAM APPROACHES

You have an important decision to make when you decide what kind of specific program approaches that you are going to take. Types of programs can be as varied as the employees you are trying to reach.

If a sizeable number of workers have reached their sixties, sessions in healthy retirement are in order. If your employees are mostly female, a class in breast self-examination is appropriate. The University System of New Hampshire offers mammography tests to female employees over 35 years of age and challenges all of its employees to be tested for high cholesterol.

Let's look at some other notable examples.

AIDS Education

Syntex, an international pharmaceutical company, has led the way with an AIDS education program for its approximately 9000 employees. Three-hour seminars for managers and supervisors focus on dealing with AIDS cases among employees. Shorter seminars for nonsupervisory personnel emphasize factual information about AIDS, the company's AIDS policy, and the fact that the disease is not transmitted through typical, casual workplace contacts.

Multiple Activities

There are many staunch advocates of the arthritis support group that is sponsored by Lawrence Livermore National Laboratory in California. Employees who suffer with arthritis share ways to cope with their condition and benefit from the chance to communicate.

That's not all that's going on at Lawrence Livermore Laboratory. Classes are offered in back care, first-aid, heart health, stress management, and smoking cessation. And if employees want referral, counseling, health screenings, or melanoma detection, they can get that, too.

STAFFED FACILITIES

For more ambitious wellness programs, you can recruit additional outside help or build facilities to house your programs. To give you an idea of some shining examples, let's preview two models of up-and-running staffed facilities.

Xerox Recreation Center

In Leesburg, Virginia, the Xerox Corporation built a Physical Fitness and Recreation Center for sales, service, and management trainees. It's hard to believe the number of healthy activities that are available to employees. There's soccer, badminton, bowling, football, softball, and basketball. Golf, handball, swimming, jogging, table games, volleyball, and racquetball are also available, and there's even a cardiovascular fitness program.

Each person who enrolls in the Xerox program begins by completing a health and fitness questionnaire, a heart attack risk chart, and a personal interview that enables a fitness specialist to design a personalized training program. Employees record their weight and heart rate throughout the program and undergo regular evaluations by a fitness specialist. Programs are continually re-evaluated and upgraded with new programs and leadership as needs and interests surface.

Release Time at Mobil

Employees of Mobil Oil's Corporate Headquarters in New York are granted release time to exercise in a spacious 2,800 square-foot fitness unit. The fitness staff designs special exercise programs for employees, and during the noon break health films are screened or guest speakers present fitness seminars. As an added encouragement, exercise logbooks are given to employees and regularly reviewed by the fitness staff.

OPERATING METHODS

The world is your oyster when it comes to selecting a wellness program for your company. Consider six options before you take the plunge:

OPTION 1   **In-house.** The do-it-yourself method. You develop, implement, and manage the program with your own employees.

OPTION 2   **Vendors.** Outside companies provide a full range of products to operate wellness programs (manuals, questionnaires, training films, health testing, speakers, and complete "packaged" programs).

OPTION 3   **Consultants.** Professionals are available locally and nationally who can help companies with most phases of program design or management. A person can be hired on a short-term basis to assist with planning or management or on a long-term basis to act as an advisor or project director.

OPTION 4   **Concessionaires.** Look for these companies to place a complete health promotion program in your facility and operate on a preset fee.

OPTION 5   **Community groups.** YMCA's, schools, and city recreation departments usually have fitness facilities and staffs that can help. Some of these groups sponsor wellness programs for companies. Just ask.

OPTION 6   **Shared programs.** Companies that want to get the most bang for their buck, work together to develop shared facilities and programs.

HEALTH RISK INVENTORIES AND APPRAISALS

INVENTORIES

Even in this new age of health awareness, many people aren't aware of all the hazards to their health. That's where personal health inventories and appraisals come in. These are instruments that help employees identify their health risks so that they can adopt healthier life styles.

Completing an inventory such as the self-test, *Healthstyle,* on pages 32 and 33 is a no-fuss first step for employees to become aware of unhealthy lifestyle patterns. *Healthstyle* is simple and short enough to be completed by everyone at an employee meeting. It's a snap for employees to test themselves, score themselves, and learn about potential health risks.

Be sure to instruct employees not to put their names on the tests so that information remains confidential. The collective information gathered about employees is valuable for the employer, because it indicates the types of programs needed.

If more than half of your employees smoke and have indicated that they want to stop, a smoking cessation seminar is sure to be a winning program choice. But you'll need to do some motivational work and provide some incentives if some of your employees smoke and tell you that they don't want to stop. In that case, Robert Orben's sign posted in a highly visible area might make some employess think twice:

"SMOKING IS THE LEADING CAUSE OF STATISTICS"

Two examples of lifestyle inventories can be found in the resource section of this book.

GIVE EMPLOYEES A HEALTH INVENTORY

APPRAISALS

One glance at the health risk appraisal from the Centers for Disease Control (pages 34 and 35) and you'll see that appraisals are more complex than health inventories. Like inventories, they indicate health risks so that people can make positive lifestyle changes before the onset of disease. Appraisals are available in a broad range of format, from paper and pencil questionnaires to interactive computer software with immediate feedback.

A health risk appraisal calculates the probability of a person becoming ill or dying from certain diseases. It's all based on health habits.

Completion of the form permits assignment of a physiological age as opposed to a chronological age. For example, a forty-eight-year-old man may have a physiological age of fifty-two, but if he starts exercising and stops smoking he could lower his physiological age to forty-six.

It's not difficult to capture employees' attention by providing specific numbers about their projected life-spans. Appraisal results often prompt people to think seriously about their health, and the way they live, many years earlier than they might have. The disadvantage to appraisals is that the calculations are based on statistical averages that may not apply to everyone.

Health risk appraisals can give a lot of mileage for their money.
Appraisals:

• provide information for consultations, referrals, and physical examinations
• allow you to plan programs that are more effective and specific
• allow you to target particular populations (i.e. smokers)
• provide a base for evaluation

Health risk appraisals and some simple body measurements are inexpensive ways to make employees aware of health risks. For more detailed information, try fitness tests, nutritional and stress assessments, and the Lifestyle Analysis Questionnaire.

Health risk appraisals are available commercially, through some universities, the Centers for Disease Control, and state health agencies. See the resource section for the address of the Centers for Disease Control in Atlanta.

HEALTHSTYLE SELF-TEST

	Almost Always	Sometimes	Almost Never
Stress Control			
1. I have a job or do other work that I enjoy.	2	1	0
2. I find it easy to relax and express my feelings freely.	2	1	0
3. I recognize early, and prepare for, events or situations likely to be stressful for me.	2	1	0
4. I have close friends, relatives, or others whom I can talk to about personal matters and call on for help when needed.	2	1	0
5. I participate in group activities (such as church and community organizations) or hobbies that I enjoy.	2	1	0
Stress Control Score:			_____
Safety			
1. I wear a seat belt while riding in a car.	2	1	0
2. I avoid driving while under the influence of alcohol and other drugs.	2	1	0
3. I obey traffic rules and the speed limit when driving.	2	1	0
4. I am careful when using potentially harmful products or substances (such as household cleaners, poisons, and electrical devices).	2	1	0
5. I avoid smoking in bed.	2	1	0
Safety Score:			_____

Cigarette Smoking

If you *never smoke*, enter a score of 10 for this section and go to the next section on *Alcohol and Drugs.*

	Almost Always	Sometimes	Almost Never
1. I avoid smoking cigarettes.	2	1	0
2. I smoke only low tar and nicotine cigarettes or I smoke a pipe or cigars.	2	1	0
Smoking Score:			_____
Exercise/Fitness			
1. I maintain a desired weight, avoiding overweight and underweight.	2	1	0
2. I do vigorous exercises for 15-30 minutes at least 3 times a week (examples include running, swimming, brisk walking).	2	1	0
3. I do exercise that enhances my muscle tone for 15-30 minutes at least 3 times a week (examples include yoga and calisthenics.)	2	1	0

Provided by ODPHP National Health Information Center

	Almost Always	Sometimes	Almost Never
Exercise/Fitness			

4. I use part of my leisure time participating in individual, family, or team activities that increase my level of fitness (such as gardening, bowling, golf, and baseball).

	2	1	0

Exercise/Fitness Score: _____

Alcohol and Drugs

1. I avoid drinking alcoholic beverages *or* I drink no more than 1 or 2 drinks a day.

	2	1	0

2. I avoid using alcohol or other drugs (especially illegal drugs) as a way of handling stressful situations or the problems in my life.

	2	1	0

3. I am careful not to drink alcohol when taking certain medicines (for example, medicine for sleeping, pain, colds, and allergies), or when pregnant.

	2	1	0

4. I read and follow the label directions when using prescribed and over-the-counter drugs.

	2	1	0

Alcohol and Drugs Score: _____

Eating Habits

1. I eat a variety of foods each day, such as fruits and vegetables, whole grain breads and cereals, lean meats, dairy products, dry peas and beans, and nuts and seeds.

	2	1	0

2. I limit the amount of fat, saturated fat, and cholesterol I eat (including fat on meats, eggs, butter, cream, shortenings, and organ meats, such as liver).

	2	1	0

3. I limit the amount of salt I eat by cooking with only small amounts, not adding salt at the table, and avoiding salty snacks.

	2	1	0

4. I avoid eating too much sugar (especially frequent snacks of sticky candy or soft drinks).

	2	1	0

Eating Habits Score: _____

WHAT YOUR SCORES MEAN TO YOU

Scores of 9 and 10—Excellent! Your answers show that you are aware of the importance of this area to your health. More important, you are putting your knowledge to work for you by practicing good health habits. As long as you continue to do, this area should not pose a serious health risk. It's likely that you are setting an example for your family and friends to follow. Since you got a very high test score on this part of the test, you may want to consider other areas where your scores indicate room for improvement.

Scores of 6 to 8—Your health practices in this area are good, but there is room for improvement. Look again at the items you answered with a "Sometimes" or "Almost Never." What changes can you make to improve your score? Even a small change can often help you achieve better health.

Scores of 3 to 5—Your health risks are showing! Would you like more information about the risks you are facing and about why it is important for you to change these behaviors? Perhaps you need help in deciding how to successfully make the changes you desire. In either case, help is available.

Scores of 0 to 2—Obviously you were concerned enough about your health to take the test, but your answers show that you may be taking serious and unnecessary risks with your health. Perhaps you are not aware of the risks and what to do about them. You can easily get the information and help you need to improve, if you wish. The next step is up to you.

34

Sample
Health Risk
Appraisal Form

Centers for Disease Control

HEALTH RISK APPRAISAL

Health Risk Appraisal is a promising health education tool that is still in the early stages of development. It is designed to show how your individual lifestyle affects your chances of avoiding the most common causes of death for a person of your age, race and sex. It also shows how much you can improve your chances by changing your harmful habits. (This particular version is not very useful for persons under 25 or over 60 years old and for persons who have had a heart attack or other serious medical problem.)

IMPORTANT: To assure protection of your privacy, do NOT put your name on this form. Make sure that you put your Health Risk Appraisal "claim check" in your wallet or other safe place and insure that the number matches the number on this form. You must present your claim check to get your computer results.

PARTICIPANT NUMBER | XX8888 | 1-6

PLEASE ENTER YOUR ANSWERS IN THE EMPTY BOXES (use numbers only)

Question	Answer	Box
1. SEX — ① Male ② Female	1	7
2. RACE ORIGIN — ① White (non-Hispanic origin) ② Black (non-Hispanic origin) ③ Hispanic ④ Asian or Pacific Islander ⑤ American Indian or Alaskan Native ⑥ Not sure	1	8
3. AGE (At Last Birthday) — Years Old	4 5	9-10
4. HEIGHT (Without Shoes) — Example: 5 foot, 7½ inches = ⑤'⑦⑤" (No Fractions)	5' 1 0"	11-13
5. WEIGHT (Without Shoes) — Pounds	1 8 5	14-16
6. TOBACCO — ① Smoker ② Ex-Smoker ③ Never Smoked	1	17

(Smokers and Ex-smokers) — Enter average number smoked per day in the last five years (ex-smokers should use the last five years before quitting.)

		Box
Cigarettes Per Day	3 0	18-19
Pipes/Cigars Per Day (Smoke Inhaled)	0 0	20-21
Pipes/Cigars Per Day (Smoke Not Inhaled)	0 0	22-23

(Ex-smokers only) Enter Number of Years Stopped Smoking (Note: Enter 1 for less than one years) — 0 0 — 24-25

7. ALCOHOL — ① Drinker ② Ex-Drinker (Stopped) ③ Non-Drinker (or drinks less than one drink per week) — 1 — 26

If you drink alcohol, enter the average number of drinks per week:

		Box
Bottles of beer per week	1 2	27-28
Glasses of wine per week	0 0	29-30
Mixed drinks or shots of liquor per week	0 0	31-32

8. DRUGS/MEDICATION   How often do you use drugs or medication which affect your mood or help you to relax?
   ① Almost every day   ② Sometimes   ③ Rarely or Never — 3 — 33

9. MILES   Per Year as a driver of a motor vehicle and/or passenger of an automobile (10,000 = average)   Thousands of miles — 1 5 0 0 0 — 34-38

10. SEAT BELT USE (percent of time used)   Example: about half the time = ☐⑤⓪ — 2 0 % — 39-41

11. PHYSICAL ACTIVITY LEVEL
   ① Level 1 - little or no physical activity
   ② Level 2 - occasional physical activity
   ③ Level 3 - regular physical activity at least 3 times per week
   — 2 — 42

NOTE: Physical activity includes work and leisure activities that require sustained physical exertion such as walking briskly, running, lifting and carrying.

12. Did either of your parents die of a heart attack before age 60?
   ① Yes, One of them   ② Yes, Both of them   ③ No   ④ Not sure — 1 — 43

13. Did your mother, father, sister or brother have diabetes?   ① Yes   ② No   ③ Not sure — 2 — 44

14. Do YOU have diabetes?   ① Yes, not controlled   ② Yes, controlled   ③ No   ④ Not sure — 3 — 45

15. Rectal problems (other than piles or hemorrhoids).

Have you had:				Box
Rectal Growth?	① Yes	② No	③ Not sure	2 — 46
Rectal Bleeding?	① Yes	② No	③ Not sure	2 — 47
Annual Rectal Exam?	① Yes	② No	③ Not sure	1 — 48

16. Has your physician ever said you have **Chronic Bronchitis or Emphysema**?	① Yes ② No ③ Not sure	**2** 49

17. Blood Pressure (If known – otherwise leave blank)

Systolic (High Number)   `1 5 0` 50-52
Diastolic (Low Number)   `9 5` 53-55

18. Fasting Cholesterol Level (If known – otherwise leave blank)   MG/DL   `[ ][ ][ ]` 56-58

19. Considering your age, how would you describe your overall physical health?
   ① Excellent   ② Good   ③ Fair   ④ Poor   **2** 59

20. In general how satisfied are you with your life?
   ① Mostly Satisfied   ② Partly Satisfied   ③ Mostly Disappointed   ④ Not Sure   **2** 60

21. In general how strong are your social ties with your family and friends?
   ① Very strong   ② About Average   ③ Weaker than average   ④ Not sure   **2** 61

22. How many hours of sleep do you usually get at night?
   ① 6 hours or less   ② 7 hours   ③ 8 hours   ④ 9 hours or more   **1** 62

23. Have you suffered a serious personal loss or misfortune in the Past Year? (For example, a job loss, disability, divorce, separation, jail term, or the death of a close person)
   ① Yes, one serious loss   ② Yes, Two or More serious losses   ③ No   **3** 63

24. How often in the Past Year did you witness or become involved in a violent or potentially violent argument?
   ① 4 or more times   ② 2 or 3 times   ③ Once or never   ④ Not sure   **3** 64

25. How many of the following things do you usually do?
- Hitch-hike or pick up hitch-hikers
- Carry a gun or knife for protection
- Keep a gun at home for protection
- Criticize or argue with strangers
- Live or work at night in a high-crime area
- Seek entertainment at night in high-crime areas or bars

   ① 3 or more   ② 1 or 2   ③ None   ④ Not sure   **2** 65

26. Have you had a hysterectomy? (Women only)
   ① Yes   ② No   ③ Not sure   `[ ]` 66

27. How often do you have Pap Smear? (Women only)
   ① At least once per year   ② At least once every 3 years   ③ More than 3 years apart
   ④ Have never had one   ⑤ Not sure   ⑥ Not applicable   `[ ]` 67

28. Was your last Pap Smear Normal? (Women only)
   ① Yes   ② No   ③ Not sure   ④ Not applicable   `[ ]` 68

29. Did your mother, sister or daughter have breast cancer? (Women only)
   ① Yes   ② No   ③ Not sure   `[ ]` 69

30. How often do you examine your breasts for lumps? (Women only)
   ① Monthly   ② Once every few months   ③ Rarely or never   `[ ]` 70

31. Have you ever completed a computerized Health Risk Appraisal Questionnaire like this one?
   ① Yes   ② No   ③ Not Sure   **2** 71

32. Current Marital Status
   ① Single (Never married)   ② Married   ③ Separated
   ④ Widowed   ⑤ Divorced   ⑥ Other   **2** 72

33. Schooling completed (One choice only)
   ① Did Not graduate from high school   ② High School
   ③ Some College   ④ College or Professional Degree   **2** 73

34. Employment Status
   ① Employed   ② Unemployed
   ③ Homemaker, Volunteer, or Student   ④ Retired, Other   **1** 74

35. Type of occupation (SKIP IF NOT APPLICABLE)
   ① Professional, Technical, Manager, Official or Proprietor   ② Clerical or Sales
   ③ Craftsman, Foreman or Operative   ④ Service or Laborer   **1** 75

36. County of Current Resident (SKIP IF NOT KNOWN)
   ⓪⑨⑨ Other   `9 9 9` 76-78

37. State of Current Residence
   ⑨⑨ Other   `9 9` 79-80)

SECTION 3

WINNING WELLNESS PROGRAM DESIGNS

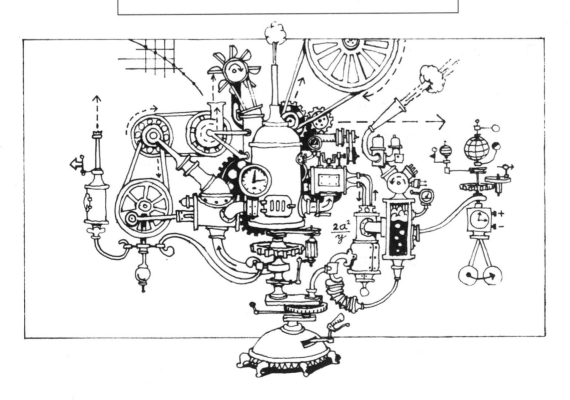

BUILD A MODEL THAT WORKS!

STRATEGIES FOR PLANNING

For effective wellness programs, incorporate the following seven strategies into your planning process.

STRATEGY 1 **Begin early...**

''Be good to yourself! Get fit with us.'' Send a message like this in a memo or post it on a bulletin board, and employees will have a difficult time passing up such an opportunity.

Start promoting your wellness program before you begin activities. Let your employees know what will be happening with:
- flyers
- posters
- meetings
- newsletter articles

If you plan to schedule hypertension education, offer blood pressure screening to stimulate employee interest. Or make cholesterol tests available to employees, and let them know cholesterol-free food information will be available in the nutrition courses.

STRATEGY 2 **Home mailings...**

Send mailings to employees with information that makes programs irresistible. Reinforcing health ideas at home packs a double-whammy in getting your message across.

STRATEGY 3 **Paycheck stuffers...**

Let your imagination soar. Write paycheck inserts that enthusiastically promote wellness. Make sure workers know that you are concerned about their health. Wellness programs can be such a vital component of your company that your employees won't want to pass up the opportunity to participate.

STRATEGY 4 **Report on the latest...**

Successful programs continually need to add fresh, new ideas of current interest. When radio, newspapers, and television break news items about health findings, follow them up with informational sessions.

When the media first reported on osteoporosis, Conoco's Health and Fitness Program responded soon afterwards by offering a program on osteoporosis for their women employees. Attendance at these sessions was overwhelming.

STRATEGY 5 **Make it lively...**

Get the facts out, but make wellness programs compelling. People like to spend time doing interesting things. Western Federal Savings (formerly Bank Western,) in Denver had rollicking success when they offered rope skipping classes, yoga demonstrations, and belly dancing lessons for employees who wanted to enjoy themselves while becoming physically fit.

STRATEGY 6 **Friendly people...**

Employees like to socialize. Capture their attention with promotional materials emphasizing opportunities to meet people with similar interests. A congenial staff that is always ready to assist employees with wellness activities is also a must.

STRATEGY 7 **Incentive awards...**

Employees get a kick out of having their health efforts acknowledged. Awards can be given for everything involving health from smoking cessation to increased activity. And there's a multitude of low-cost incentive awards such as:
- crests
- t-shirts
- lapel pins
- coffee mugs
- certificates

Incentives for walking programs can be as simple as establishing mileage markers along a walking path.

At the Macalloy Corporation, a small steel mill in Charleston, South Carolina, all employees who control their hypertension are awarded ''I Did It'' stickers as incentives to be placed on their hard hats.

For more costly awards give:
- fitness club memberships
- trips to health conferences
- tuition for health-related courses

NINE CORE
WELLNESS PROGRAMS

Now you can take a giant step and start planning some specific wellness programs of your own. This section will help by presenting information about nine of the core health risks you're likely to encounter among employees. Informative facts, fascinating tidbits, ideas for educational seminars, and highlights from companies involved in specific programs are at your fingertips to make your planning amazingly simple. And if that's not enough, a listing of dozens of other programs follows at the end of this section. (There's so much information, the program will practically run itself.)

CORE #1   NUTRITION EDUCATION

Fact, Not Fiction

- Few people take the time to sit down to three square meals a day anymore. One-fourth of all Americans eat breakfast in their cars. The American Dietetic Association estimates that instead of three meals per day, the average person has contact with food 20 times during the day. The rise of fast food service, together with changes in social and working patterns, have created a new eating phenomenon in our society.

- The problem with modern-day eating is that more than one-half of the calories consumed come from fat, sugar, and alcohol; all are empty sources of nutrition. Chips, cookies, and sweet rolls often replace some nutritious foods that contribute to good health.

- Nutrition is not just a concern for people who are underweight or overweight. Five of the ten leading causes of death are diet-related. Employees who make wise food choices that meet their nutritional needs do a better job preparing their bodies to handle the daily stresses of living and work.

Nutrabreak

In Kentucky, the Lexington-Fayette County Health Department established "Nutrabreak," a program to encourage its 320 employees to eat more nutritious snacks and to learn about nutrition. Every Wednesday morning, the nutrition staff provides low-cost nutritious snacks along with recipes, educational handouts, and verbal food-fact information. Posters and announcements, at staff meetings and in the department newsletter, promote program participation. The Nutrabreak Program is offered in conjunction with Break Walking and Fresh Approach Lunches to help department workers improve their own health and become more effective health educators.

Educational Sessions

You can promote proper nutrition and help employees live longer, more productive lives by scheduling these effective learning sessions. Note the month that you want to schedule each session. Of course, there's one month off for good behavior.

Month of Program	Topics
_____	Label literacy
_____	Low-fat cooking
_____	Buying food wisely
_____	Healthy trends in eating
_____	Healthy cooking techniques
_____	Nutrition for busy families
_____	Good choices when eating out
_____	Healthy food choices and habits
_____	Nutritious meal planning on a low budget
_____	Learning about salt, fiber, sugar, calories, and cholesterol
_____	Food to reduce risks of cancer, diabetes, heart disease, digestive disorders, and high blood pressure.

Tantalizing Activities

When employers want to help workers improve their nutrition, there are countless things that they can do. Something as simple as posting the calories contained in lunchroom meals or making fruit available in the break room can affect employee health. Scherer Brothers Lumber Company in Minneapolis, Minnesota, serves free, nutritious hot noon meals to all of its employees as a means of bolstering nutrition.

Try some of these inspirational activities to promote better employee nutritional status. Add two activities of your own to make a baker's dozen.

Month of Activity	Activities
_____	Promote healthy lunch box days.
_____	Offer a salad bar in the cafeteria.
_____	Make popcorn or fruit available for healthy snacks.
_____	Print and distribute healthy-food shopping lists.
_____	Serve juices and healthy, low-calorie snacks at meetings.
_____	Provide salt and sugar substitutes in the cafeteria and break rooms.
_____	Buy a small microwave and refrigerator to encourage healthier bag lunches.
_____	Make a scale available in a private location so employees can weigh themselves.
_____	Make healthy food choices available in vending machines (nuts and fruits instead of candy).
_____	Post salt, caloric, and cholesterol contents of items in the vending machines (one small package of candy = 240 calories).
_____	Offer Culinary Hearts Kitchen Course, 6 weeks of classes sponsored by the American Heart Association.
_____	(Add your own activities).
	_____
_____	_____

See the resource section of this book to find additional information on nutrition.

CORE #2   HYPERTENSION

Lockheed Shipbuilders

When a high blood pressure control program was started for the predominantly male employees of Lockheed Shipbuilding and Construction Company in Seattle, Washington, initial screening showed that approximately 30 percent of the participants had high blood pressure or a history of blood pressure problems. This alarming percentage compared to 20 percent of the general adult population. It was clear that Lockheed's employees could benefit from on-site education and intervention.

After Lockheed's activities of publicity, education, screening, referral, follow-up and evaluation, a whopping 54.2 percent of their employees showed improved blood pressure levels and 40.8 percent brought their blood pressure under control. This is the kind of success that people can live with!

The Silent Killer

Screening has detected millions of people in the United States with high blood pressure. Known as the ''silent killer,'' hypertension (high blood pressure) claims more victims each year. High blood pressure is linked with a higher incidence of illness and death. Although hypertension usually does not manifest symptoms, detecting the disease is easy and relatively inexpensive.

Hypertension Education and Activities

The following topics will help you begin planning a hypertension program. Indicate your program schedule by placing the numbers 1 through 7 opposite the topics.

_____ Exercise
_____ Smoking cessation
_____ Stress management
_____ Food and alcohol awareness
_____ Weight and cholesterol control
_____ Worksite treatment and follow-up
_____ Blood pressure screening and referral

The American Heart Association is an excellent source for obtaining hypertension materials both for professionals and employees. You can contact your local chapter for advice or assistance with screening activities. Turn to the resource section of this book for addresses of agencies that have additional information.

CORE #3   STRESS MANAGEMENT

Enlightening Facts

• You may have heard about the employees who became discouraged about stress. All summer they went to workshops learning how to deal with stress. And at the same time their managers went to conventions learning how to create it.

• The greatest toll from stress may not come from the death of a spouse, a move to a different city, or other major changes, but from minor annoyances experienced in daily living and work. A study conducted by the University of California/Berkeley found that relatively unimportant hassles take a greater toll on health than larger life traumas.

Stress-Related Cases

Let's look at some examples of stress.

• A middle-aged switchboard operator returns to work after hospitalization for a mental collapse. She has difficulty keeping up with the demanding pace of her job.

• A young assembly worker is taken to the hospital emergency room after a bad experience with drugs. He says he can't cope with the tedium of his job without cocaine.

• An older executive secretary is under doctor's care for migraine headaches. Her doctor feels that her condition is aggravated by her job responsibilities.

These employees are all suffering from stress-related illnesses. When stress is poorly managed, it can cause serious sickness. It can also have major consequences on a person's ability to function at work.

Worksite Stress Reduction

Although researchers don't completely understand stress, they do know effective coping techniques for dealing with it. Two companies in the midwest are actively involved in reducing stress for their employees.

• The Faultless Starch Bon Ami Company of Kansas City, Missouri, advocates that its employees engage in meditation to reduce stress and anticipates that future health insurance premiums will be reduced because of its use.

• The Ford Motor Company's corporate headquarters in Dearborn, Michigan, invites employees to use its recreation department several times a week for instruction in stress-reducing yoga and transcendental meditation.

Learning Seminars

Schedule these stress management sessions on a priority basis of 1-15, with a rating of 1 identifying the first valuable seminar that you plan to schedule.

Rating	Seminar Topics
_____	Diet and nutrition
_____	Communication skills
_____	The quieting response
_____	Assertiveness training
_____	Effective time management
_____	Self-monitoring techniques
_____	Support system development
_____	Substance abuse and stress
_____	"Inoculating" against stress
_____	Coping with occupational stressors
_____	Risk factors and response to stress
_____	Self-regulation techniques (imaging)
_____	Exercising to reduce stress
_____	Irrational beliefs and psychotic stress
_____	Personality type and predisposition to stress

Local mental health associations provide stress-reduction programs that can be offered to employees for a small fee. Other helpful information can be obtained by contacting the agencies listed in the resource section of this book.

To obtain an informative book on stress management, use the information in the back of this book to order the Crisp Publication, *Mental Fitness* by Merrill Raber, M.S.W., Ph.D. and George Dyck, M.D.

CORE #4   FITNESS AND EXERCISE

Fitness Facts

- Our bodies wear out faster from disease than from use, yet when it comes to aerobic exercise, most workers say ''no'' to running, walking, swimming, or other strenuous activity. The Centers for Disease Control report that only eight percent of adults age 18-65 participate in recommended vigorous 20-minute exercise three times a week.
- Exercise aids sleep, tones major muscles, helps reduce stress, renews one's sense of well-being, and protects the body from cardiovascular disease. Exercise increases the body's ability to fight disease, which is important because the decline of the immune system appears to be the major factor in human aging and life span.
- To avoid becoming overly fatigued, employees need a work capacity four to five times as great as the work they currently perform. Is it any wonder that employers are concerned about the fitness of their employees?

Workplace Fitness

Employees at The Alco Container Corporation know exactly where they're going when they head out for noontime walks. The company provides easy-to-follow maps that indicate semi-hilly and hilly routes and the time-frames to complete them within the lunch hour.

The South Carolina State Board of Nursing schedules activities according to the seasons. They sponsor a daily, two-mile morning walk in the summer and noontime walks in the spring and fall for all interested employees.

Other companies promote wellness by installing bike racks and cheering on employees who walk or ride bikes to work. Workers are encouraged to park at the far end of parking lots, take the stairs instead of elevators, and participate in morning and afternoon stretch breaks at their desks. Some companies make available aerobic exercise cassettes and videotapes that employees can use at work or at home. Others promote wellness by arranging discounts for employees and families at stores that sell athletic shoes and apparel.

When employees of a store fixtures manufacturer, the Lozier Corporation, swim 50 miles, bike 500 miles, skate 250 miles, or walk or run 100 miles, they receive a membership in the company's distinctive Century Club. And at Bonnie Bell Company in Lakewood, Ohio, regular exercise translates into financial incentives for employees. Bonnie Bell boasts exercise classes three times weekly, tennis courts (with lessons), and a jogging path with exercise stations along the way.

Learning Seminars

To identify your priorities, rate these seminar subjects from 1-6:

____ Relaxation techniques

____ Your target heart rate

____ Maintaining proper posture

____ Avoiding dangerous exercise

____ Getting motivated and sticking with it

____ Developing the three basic components of fitness: aerobic capacity, flexibility, tone and endurance

Healthy Activities

Even if your company doesn't have a formal wellness program, you may still be involved in some of the following activities. Check ☑ the ones you are already doing and those you plan to introduce:

Already Doing	Will Do	Activities
☐	☐	Aerobic classes
☐	☐	Workplace bowling teams
☐	☐	Group exercise sessions
☐	☐	Maintaining a garden plot
☐	☐	Lessons in individual sports
☐	☐	Group health club membership
☐	☐	Recreation classes and leagues
☐	☐	Cycling, running, and jogging clubs
☐	☐	Workplace challenge volleyball teams
☐	☐	Group court time for tennis, handball, and racquetball
☐	☐	Employee trips: skiing, hiking, camping, canoeing, cycling, or backpacking

Although you may have made very few check marks above, your company's employees may still be getting a lot of exercise. After all, people are always pushing their luck, jumping to conclusions, dodging responsibilities, flying off the handle, carrying things too far, and running around in circles!

Look in the resource section of this book under "Fitness and Exercise" for additional sources of information.

CORE #5 SMOKING CESSATION

Some Hard Facts

Concerned with liability and increasing evidence about the damaging effects of secondary smoke, employers have stepped up efforts to ban smoking in the workplace. After the Surgeon General's report warned that secondary smoke—what nonsmoking workers breathe when their colleagues smoke—causes an increased risk of cancer and other diseases, momentum for company action surged.

• The U.S. Department of Health, Education, and Welfare reports that smokers spend an average of one hour a day or about four work weeks each year practicing their habit. Smoking-related illnesses cost employers a walloping $25 billion each year in employee absences and another $13 billion in medical care. Surveys suggest that smoking bans and tougher on-the-job restrictions can help smokers reduce their use of tobacco.

• Smoking is the single most preventable cause of death, yet one-third of the adults in America continue to smoke. The mortality rate from lung cancer is rising more rapidly for women than for men and is expected to continue climbing in the next decade since women give up smoking less readily than men. The majority of adults (80 percent or higher) are aware that emphysema, chronic bronchitis, and cancer of the lung, larynx, and esophagus are associated with smoking. Only about one-third correctly associate bladder cancer with smoking.

• The number of cigarettes smoked per day also directly affects cholesterol level. On the average, cholesterol levels rise a half a point for each cigarette smoked. But when smokers quit, cholesterol levels quickly come down.

Cessation Programs

The toll of smoking in terms of human suffering and the economy is staggering. The good news is that every time the risks of smoking are publicized, more smokers motivate themselves to give up the habit. Most smokers have either tried to quit smoking or want to quit. And that's where employers can help employees kick a deadly habit by offering in-house commercial, and incentive programs, community clinics, and packaged materials.

In-House Programs

Companies can organize successful smoking cessation programs by sponsoring informational and motivational presentations by health care personnel, offering individual and group counseling, and distributing "how-to-quit" materials. Programs are often too expensive to develop in-house, because of the intensive staff support needed for employees who seek assistance with smoking problems.

Commercial Smoking Cessation Programs

Let your fingers do the walking through the yellow pages, and you'll have no trouble locating commercial smoking cessation programs. Companies can be found in most areas; their costs tend to vary widely.

Incentive Programs

Often spelling the difference between success and failure, incentive programs are as varied as smokers themselves. A simple "I QUIT" button might be all the incentive needed to motivate an employee to stop smoking. Some companies reimburse employees with the total cost of smoking cessation programs if they stay tobacco-free for a year or longer. Other companies split the cost of the program with employees.

Community Clinics

Companies can call on community service agencies such as the American Cancer Society, American Lung Association, and local health departments to provide smoking cessation clinics for little or no cost.

Packaged Materials

Look for films, videotapes, audio cassettes, and publications as motivational resources for smoking cessation or to supplement smoking cessation programs.

Smoke-Free GTE

When GTE-Northwest in Everett, Washington, made the decision to go smoke-free, they offered employees several smoking cessation options including a self-help package, a class-structured program, additional group cessation classes, or a $25 rebate towards another program of their choice. Very few employees took advantage of the rebate, but 400 workers participated in various group cessation programs. Another 200 participated in the ''Free and Clear'' self-help program.

At the end of the year, GTE-Northwest employees numbered 204 new non-smokers. The company estimates that it saves $622 a year for each nonsmoker. The smoking cessation effort saved the company nearly $12,000, less $4,000 to provide the programs. Health care providers indicate that in other companies the cost of each smoker is estimated as high as $1,500 more per year than for nonsmokers.

Additional Avenues

In addition to providing incentives and education, consider augmenting your smoking cessation effort by:
- removing cigarette machines
- implementing bans on smoking
- writing smoking policies to respect the rights
  of smokers and nonsmokers

Local units of the American Cancer Society and American Lung Association publish booklets that contain policy guidelines, employee survey forms, and suggested wording for smoking policies.

Ford Motor Company

The United States' second largest industrial company, Ford Motor Company, is going all out by banning smoking in all areas where not expressly permitted by union contract. The ban applies to the company's top executives and directors as well as rank and file workers and was suggested by the employees themselves.

Nonsmoking Activities

Member companies of the Wellness Council of the Midlands (WELCOM) have compiled these winning ideas for employers that want to help workers stop smoking:

- Install smoke removal machines.
- Participate in the Great American Smokeout every November by contacting your local unit of the American Cancer Society.
- Conduct your own smokeout day or designate one day per week as a nonsmoking day.
- Provide smoking survival stations equipped with carrot sticks, sugarless gum, and sunflower seeds for smokeout participants.
- Serve breakfast to smokeout participants. Ask them to leave their cigarettes on a table when they leave.
- Nonsmokers can "adopt" smokers and extend moral support during smokeout day.
- Contribute to the American Lung Association in tribute to employees who have stopped smoking.
- Remove ashtrays, keep them clean, or fill them with wrapped candy.
- Display posters extolling the benefits of not smoking. Many posters are available at no cost from federal or voluntary health agencies.
- Reward employees who have stopped smoking for a designated length of time.
- Do some brainstorming and add more trailblazing ideas of your own below:

_____

_____

Smoking cessation materials including kits, pamphlets, and brochures are available from the centers listed in the resource section.

CORE #6   ALCOHOL AND DRUG PREVENTION

Frightening Facts

- Drinkers pay a steep excise tax for the alcohol they buy. But it doesn't begin to cover the actual costs to society in terms of their illness and medical expenses. The excise tax on an ounce of alcohol is 23 cents, but the cost to society is an alarming 48 cents an ounce.
- Advertising often seeks to make alcohol consumption fun or glamorous. In one evening of television viewing, it's not uncommon to see ''lite'' beer touted as the drink of choice. Alcohol plays a major role in American culture.
- The U.S. Department of Human Services estimates that the average alcoholic cheats his employer out of approximately 25 percent of his salary each year through tardiness, lower productivity, and absenteeism. Yet, few alcoholics can consciously recognize that their dependency problems affect their work, particularly as the dependency problems become more extreme.

Helpful Seminars

If your company does not have an Employee Assistance Program or is not ready to develop one, assistance can be given to employees by offering informational seminars on alcohol and drug awareness. Some of your employees may be more responsive to information if they attend a small group session where they can discuss their concerns. To aid in your planning, check ☑ the appropriate space for small or large group sessions.

Small group	Large group	Alcohol/Drug Prevention Topics
_____	_____	Social attitudes
_____	_____	Withdrawal and relapse
_____	_____	Recognition of being addicted
_____	_____	Craving and addiction tolerance
_____	_____	Adolescent drinking and drug use
_____	_____	Interactions of medications and alcohol
_____	_____	Use of prescription and nonprescription drugs

Prevention Activities

Addiction is a complex subject, but some of the ways you can help employees avoid or overcome it are quite simple:

1. Write a policy regarding the use and serving of alcohol at company-sponsored events.
2. At social events, refrain from serving alcohol, or serve a variety of appealing nonalcoholic beverages as an alternative.
3. To familiarize employees with Alcoholics Anonymous and make it easier for them to attend, invite an AA group to use your facility for meetings.
4. Before holidays, distribute nonalcoholic drink recipes to employees.
5. To create awareness about alcohol problems, employees of Central States Health and Life Company of Omaha suggest that workers produce and act in a psychodrama about alcohol and its devastating effects on a person's family and work.

Other helpful alcohol and drug prevention sources are listed in the resource section of this book. For an excellent book on chemical dependency, refer to the Crisp Publication, *Job Performance and Chemical Dependency* by Robert Maddux and Lynda Voorhees. For ordering information, see the information in the back of this book.

HAVE A WRITTEN POLICY ABOUT ALCOHOL

CORE #7   WEIGHT CONTROL

Edifying Facts

- When nutritionists recently decided to find out how much running is required to burn off various fast food items, they discovered that you would have to run 10.5 miles to burn off the calories in a double superburger with cheese, and four miles for a chocolate milkshake. Exercise does expend calories, but when people really want to lose weight they generally need to combine working out with eating less.
- The average person consumes more calories at lunchtime than he requires to perform the physical activities of an eight-hour work day. An employee who works at a desk uses 400-550 calories for on-the-job activities. With a superburger, shake, and french fries containing about 1100 calories, it's no wonder that 64 percent of American adults are overweight. At no time in the history of our country has obesity been so epidemic.
- Many experts believe that repeated dieting is the main reason so many people in the U.S. are fat today. Doctors at the University of Washington found that dieting makes your body think that it's starving, so it slows down to save energy. And even when the diet's over, body metabolism never returns to normal because the body stores fat more efficiently. The ironic result is that chronic dieters often have the hardest time losing weight!

Larimer County Shape-Up Contests

Innovative ways abound when employers want to help workers with weight control. The Larimer County Health Department in Ft. Collins, Colorado, sponsors Shape-Up Weight Loss Contests for employees. During 12-week competitions, participants pay an entry fee and form teams of five employees each.

Participants weigh in weekly and receive printed information on exercise, nutrition, and weight control. Each team's progress toward their weight loss goal is posted on a weekly chart. The winning team has the fun and good fortune of collecting all the entry fees! The program is open to all adult employees who weigh more than their recommended weight.

Weighty Seminars

Companies can also sponsor informational sessions to help employees with weight control. Review the 13 topics that follow and check ☑ three or four for introducing seminars in weight control. If your employees are responsive to the first sessions, you'll know you can plan an additional three or four that will be well attended.

- ☐ Exercise
- ☐ Fad dieting
- ☐ Changing behavior
- ☐ Stress and hunger
- ☐ Building a support system
- ☐ Eating out, having guests
- ☐ Coping with hunger feelings
- ☐ Long-term weight maintenance
- ☐ Food shopping and meal planning
- ☐ Nutritional needs and how they change
- ☐ Vacations, special events, holidays
- ☐ Desired body weight and goal-setting
- ☐ Weight control and self-responsibility

Refer to the resource section of this book to find more sources of information on food, exercise, nutrition, maintenance, and action plans.

POOR EATING HABITS CAN BE MODIFIED

CORE #8   SAFETY AND ACCIDENT PREVENTION

Eye-Opening Information

Look in your own back yard and you'll probably find some excellent reasons to start a safety program. Thousands of on-the-job employee deaths and millions of disabling injuries occur every year. The work that is being performed, or the workplace itself, often creates many health and safety hazards.

Test your safety awareness by identifying the following three statements as ''TRUE'' or ''FALSE.''

TRUE   **FALSE**

_____   _____   It is safer and healthier to work in an office than outdoors or in a factory.

False. An office is not always the safest place to work. Health hazards in the office stem from poor lighting, indoor air pollution, poorly designed furniture and equipment, and even long hours at the video display terminal.

_____   _____   Workplace hazards readily produce identifiable symptoms.

False again. Employees may not recognize as work-related subtle problems that can develop over a long period of time. If a wobbly chair breaks and an employee falls to the floor, any consequent injury is recognized right away. But a wobbly chair can cause back strain a worker does not usually recognize immediately. When a backache develops, the employee may not relate the pain to the chair.

_____   _____   Stress is not always recognized as a health and safety issue in the workplace.

True. People assume that since automated machinery and computers do a lot of the work, jobs should be easier and less stressful. Not so. Read on.

Stress Issues

- When the Communication Workers of America conducted a study with female telephone employees in North Carolina, they found that 20 percent suffered from chest pain after working more than four hours at video display terminals. These employees experience chest pain at four times the rate found in the general population.
- The following issues affect employee health and safety:
  —boredom
  —job burnout
  —''impossible'' deadlines
  —constant deadline pressure
  —crowded work spaces
  —fear of unemployment
  —erratic work schedules
  —workaholic syndrome

Psychological stress on the job causes accidents and occupational-related diseases, yet the link between job and illness is often unrecognized and unreported. To reduce job stress, it is sometimes necessary to identify the stress factors and redesign jobs to give employees more control.

ANYONE CAN STRESS OUT FROM TIME TO TIME

Ergonomics

The science of matching people, machines, and environment, called ergonomics, has proved that more efficient design of offices and equipment can:
- decrease employee turnover
- improve work productivity
- increase work performance

People who work in ergonomically designed offices usually do a better job, are happier, and are less likely to leave their job. But if workers do leave, it is much easier to attract new employees.

Choices of color, music, and lighting can do more than cheer up working areas, according to interior design experts. Their appropriate use can also reduce stress, improve safety, and increase productivity.

The Wrong Colors

When a Volkswagon plant in West Germany experienced too many work-related injuries, design experts noticed that the colors in the plant were too soft. Employees were having trouble staying alert and awake while working. When the colors in the plant were changed to more vivid primary colors, the injury rate dropped dramatically.

WORKPLACES CAN BE TOO RELAXING!

Absenteeism and Accidents

Did you know that you can use absenteeism* information to prevent injuries? Robert J. Will, President of Rate Consultants, Inc., reports a connection between workplace injuries and absenteeism. Employees with poor attitudes toward their companies and its safety rules are more likely to be injured on the job than satisfied employees. They are also likely to be absent more frequently in a six month period prior to an injury.

Companies may be able to prevent injuries or reduce them by:
- noting rises in absenteeism
- increasing safety instruction when absenteeism has risen
- providing close supervision for workers with higher absenteeism
- helping employees work through problems that are creating stress and resultant absenteeism

Worksite Health and Safety Survey

Take a survey of your workplace to identify areas that may be contributing to health risks and accidents. Place an (X) next to those factors that may pose a risk to your employees.

- ☐ noise
- ☐ colors
- ☐ furniture
- ☐ supply areas
- ☐ working spaces
- ☐ work organization
- ☐ worker absenteeism
- ☐ machines and equipment
- ☐ video display terminals
- ☐ ventilation and air quality
- ☐ work safety policies and procedures
- ☐ ammenities (lounges, lunchrooms, bathrooms)
- ☐ health symptoms of employees (Are employees experiencing symptoms of itching, allergies, or irritated eyes that might indicate health hazards?)

A more complete worksite survey can be found in the book *Office Work Can Be Dangerous to Your Health* by Jeanne Stellman, Ph.D. and Mary Sue Henifin, M.P.H.

---

* An excellent book on this topic is *Attacking Absenteeism* by Lynn Tylczak which may be ordered from the back of this book.

Fire Safety

Don't overlook another major employee concern in worksite health promotion: fire safety. Fire policies and procedures are similar to those developed for schools, except that the rationale for them is possibly better understood by adults. A first grader was talking about a recent fire in her school. "I knew it was going to happen," she said. "We had been practicing for it all year."

Hazard Map

Making a hazard map will help you target specific work areas that may be hazardous to employees. Draw a diagram of each work area, mark the hazards, and recommend changes that are needed.

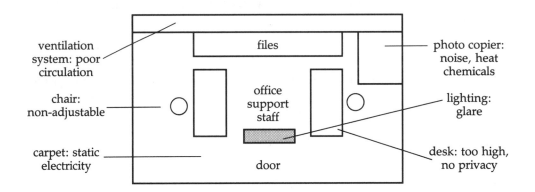

Accident Prevention Activities

Be your own safety engineer and add to the accident prevention activities that are listed below.

1. Post the number of days since the last worker injury.

2. Show employees the cost savings for each of them if the number of injuries is reduced by a certain percentage.

3. Start an incentive program if accidents and injury rates are high. Give recognition to employees who haven't had injuries within a specified time period.

4. Correct potentially hazardous problems. If an employee's unstable chair is not fixed, the company may end up paying the high price of workers' compensation for absenteeism due to back pain.

5. (Your idea) _____

6. (Your idea) _____

A Hazard-Filled World

Offices are not the only places to find occupational hazards. It's no secret that people who work in factories are sometimes exposed to radiation, toxic chemicals, excessive noise, or vibration that can cause disease and birth defects in unborn children. Workers in mining, agriculture, and construction industries are more likely to die from work-related injuries than other employees.

Home and Car Dangers

Your home can also be hazardous to your health. Most adults do not know the temperature of the hot water in their homes or the temperature that it takes for scald injuries to occur. About two-fifths of homes do not have a working smoke detector. And when traveling from work to home, only about one-third of adults wear seat belts when in their cars.

Safety Seminars

Employees who are protected from hazards in the workplace, in cars, and at home have health and safety working as a basic component in their lives. You can help even more by providing informational sessions that will help prevent accidents. If you have available space, you can add variety and interest by scheduling seminars in two or three different locations at the worksite.

Month of Program	Prevention Topics
_____	Back care
_____	First-aid
_____	Self-defense
_____	Seat belt use
_____	Heimlich maneuver
_____	Defensive driving
_____	Correct lifting techniques
_____	Strength and endurance exercises
_____	Accident/fire emergency procedures
_____	Creating a safe working environment
_____	Cardiopulmonary resuscitation (CPR)

The resource section lists sources for additional safety and accident prevention posters, brochures, and information.

CORE #9   EMPLOYEE ASSISTANCE PROGRAMS

Illuminating Information

- A 53-year-old cashier is in danger of losing her job because of excessive absenteeism. The reason: an aging father at her home needs care because he is senile.
- A 27-year-old accountant continues to fall asleep at her desk during working hours. She is a single mother who is attempting to work two full-time jobs to pay off debts.
- A 31-year-old salesman is exhibiting wide mood swings and irritability while at work. The cause: nighttime drinking.

Such situations as these are not unusual in the workplace. Tardiness, absenteeism, reduced performance, and decreased productivity are often the price that companies pay when employees have personal problems.

Some companies are tackling these problems with Employee Assistance Programs (EAPs). Unlike wellness programs with a preventive approach, EAPs are considered a health promotion essential because they address existing problems. Companies have discovered that it costs less to help employees cope with personal problems than to fire them and repeat the hiring, training, and termination cycle. EAPs are designed to provide professional and confidential help to workers whose job performance is or may be adversely affected by such problems as:
- death
- aging
- violence
- legal issues
- family trouble
- drugs and alcohol
- emotional difficulties

Formally defined systems provide a way to intervene when an employee fails to recognize the need for help. They offer trained professionals when assistance is needed and allow a company to keep records of the types, numbers, and outcomes of problems that are handled.

Success Story

- EAP's success rate of rehabilitating troubled employees has been as high as 82 percent, according to William May, former CEO of the American Can Company. The figure shows a large percentage of people rehabilitated, but it doesn't show the thousands of dollars saved through increased productivity and the avoidance of training costs from employee turnover.

Types of Employee Assistance Programs

You'll need to keep a critical eye and a hand on the pocketbook when considering options for EAP programs.

OPTION 1 **In-house services.** Staffing can be full-time or part-time. When the position is part-time, the EAP employee usually does not assume other job responsibilities because of the need to protect confidentiality. EAP staff needs to have the ability to establish rapport with all types of people and to be knowledgeable about clinical problems, assessment techniques, and appropriate referral sources.

OPTION 2 **Contract for service.** Stretch your purchasing power and investigate the increasing number of independent providers of EAP services. Some hospitals provide Employee Assistance Programs on a contractual basis.

OPTION 3 **Combination design.** Think about looking for an external provider or consultant to work with your in-house staff on EAP program development, implementation, or management.

OPTION 4 **Consortium.** Several companies can combine forces to operate an EAP that serves all their employees.

Organizations that can provide further EAP assistance are listed in the resource section of this book.

DOZENS OF IDEAS

Are you still looking for additional ideas for health information sessions for your employees? The list of possible topics is virtually endless! If you want to schedule one topic each month, there's more than enough on the list below for a two-year period. And that doesn't include the group of topics that have been outlined above.

Jot down the month and the year that you want to schedule each topic, and you have taken your first step in health education planning.

Month	Year	Seminar Topics
_____	_____	Eye Care
_____	_____	First-Aid
_____	_____	Back Care
_____	_____	Foot Care
_____	_____	Skin Care
_____	_____	Immunization
_____	_____	Mental Health
_____	_____	General Health
_____	_____	Chronic Disease
_____	_____	Elderly Parents
_____	_____	Staying Healthy
_____	_____	Heimlich Maneuver
_____	_____	Handling Depression
_____	_____	Communicable Diseases
_____	_____	When To Call A Doctor
_____	_____	Cancer Risk Reduction
_____	_____	Working Mother's Issues
_____	_____	Breast Self-Examination
_____	_____	Preparing for Retirement
_____	_____	Dental Disease Prevention

Month	Year	Seminar Topics
_____	_____	Pregnancy and Infant Care
_____	_____	Testicular Self-Examination
_____	_____	Heart Attack Risk Reduction
_____	_____	Concerns about Child Rearing
_____	_____	Self-Care for Common Ailments
_____	_____	Health Services and Resources
_____	_____	Cardiopulmonary Resuscitation
_____	_____	Selecting Physicians/Hospitals
_____	_____	Concerns about Elderly Parents
_____	_____	Wise Use of Health Care Benefits
_____	_____	Buying Generic Drugs/Drug Reactions
_____	_____	Disabilities and Sensory Impairments
_____	_____	AIDs and Other Sexually Transmitted Diseases
_____	_____	Special Disease Awareness: Sickle Cell Anemia

SECTION 4

NO COST, LOW COST HEALTH PROMOTION IDEAS

"I HAVE A SMALL LIST OF HEALTH PROMOTION IDEAS"

LOW COST, NO COST HEALTH PROMOTION IDEAS

SCREENING PROGRAMS

You'll chart a healthy course for employees when you give them the opportunity to have medical screenings. And that's just part of the story. Screenings for cholesterol, glaucoma, diabetes, high blood pressure, and sickle cell anemia become catalysts that interest more workers in wellness. Local voluntary agencies are usually happy to screen for disease at no charge.

RESOURCE LIBRARY

Develop a lending library and you'll give employees the opportunity to explore health interests on their own. Plan to include:
- cookbooks
- health books
- health magazines
- self-help books and cassettes
- health booklets and brochures
- newspaper and magazine articles on wellness
- videos on health, nutrition, and fitness

Government and voluntary agencies are a rich source for free resource materials. If your budget permits, purchase video and cassette players that workers can borrow.

SUPPORT GROUPS

Form support groups for employees who are dieters, ex-smokers, and bad-back sufferers, or who are concerned about children or elderly parents. Support groups members can take turns making presentations and being responsible for the gatherings.

In support groups anything goes. They can vary in format, support, numbers, duration, and frequency of meetings. But all have the same objective: providing support and understanding to their members.

VENDING MACHINES

Dazzle your health-conscious workers by making healthy foods available in snack machines. Nuts, juices, yogurt, low-fat milk, sunflower seeds, and fresh and dried fruits are nutritious, delicious alternatives to cupcakes and candy bars. Think of it: your employees may become so healthy and trim, they'll start competing in body beautiful contests!

CAFETERIA/DINING ROOM

Offer nutritious foods, and post their calorie and cholesterol contents.

Each day the Continental Bank in Chicago offers a different ''wellness meal'' that has proved to be an all-time favorite with employees. Some companies make attractive discounts available on their more nutritious food items.

NEWSLETTER

Don't rely on word-of-mouth popularity for your health promotion program. Publish a wellness newsletter or include upbeat articles and health columns in existing company publications.

BREAKS

To give your employees a new lease on life, play a music tape for ''no-sweat'' bending and stretching exercises during an 8-10 minute break. Fitness Canada calls this the ''foot in the door approach.'' If employees start exercising during breaks, they may well move on to bigger and better things in the world of fitness on their own time.

Add some zip to the traditional coffee break by offering juice or fruit. Make sure that reading materials on health, fitness, and nutrition are available in the break area.

ACTIVITY CLUBS

Employees will be delighted if you encourage those with similar interests to form clubs. The groups can organize at the workplace and participate in the club activities during the evening or on weekends.

Need ideas for clubs? Suggest activities like hiking, skiing, cycling, running, jogging, walking, climbing, gardening, backpacking, scuba diving, and ballroom dancing. Whatever gets the body moving deserves your support.

CLASSES

Ready for a refreshing change-of-pace? At regular intervals offer group exercise classes that don't require a special space or shower facilities. Look for an employee or family member who is interested in leading some of the class sessions and is qualified to do so.

Perk up the class selections by offering yoga, jazzercise, belly dancing, disco dancing, or low-impact aerobics. Rotate program responsibilities among interested employees or departments. Your employees will enjoy the challenge.

LUNCHTIME

Even peanut butter sandwiches will be mouthwatering if you schedule engrossing "Lunch and Learn" seminars about health topics. Guided walking tours or routes that have been mapped for walks during the noon hour can healthfully spice up the midday break for the active lunch bunch.

WELLNESS WEEK

Plan a wellness week and your employees will experience an adventure in learning when they participate in awards, screenings, presentations, a fun run, smokeout day, low-calorie cooking contest, wellness poster contest, exercise demonstrations, and Heimlich maneuver demonstrations. If you offer enough variety, everyone will want to get into the act.

THEME WEEKS

Focus on a particular subject for a week and offer a range of activities. For example, an Exercise Week could feature a film on aerobics, a lecture on running, a noontime group hike, and an employee walking day.

PAYROLL INSERTS

Good news! Payroll stuffers are a great way to make employees health conscious. Local voluntary agencies, government agencies, and dental and medical associations are usually willing to make literature available for company distribution. You'll find a lot of information out there without having to do much digging.

Send out inserts on:
- smoking
- diabetes
- exercise
- eye care
- skin care
- back care
- first aid
- dental care
- skin cancer
- immunizations
- seat belt use
- lung disorders
- defensive driving
- Heimlich maneuver
- stress management
- high blood pressure
- heart risk reduction
- cancer risk reduction
- healthy food selection
- cardiopulmonary resuscitation

**USE YOUR IMAGINATION FOR
WAYS TO SHARE HEALTH IDEAS**

SPECIAL EVENTS AND COMPETITIONS

Countless hours of healthy activities are provided when employees are actively involved in special events and competitions. Employee tennis, volleyball, walkathons, softball tournaments, stair climbing contests, and cross-country ski runs will delight the more adventurous contingent of workers.

POSTER CAMPAIGNS

Watch posters go to work for you by spreading the good news about wellness. Change health messages frequently and display posters in hallways, elevators, break rooms, and dining areas.

PRESENTATIONS

Knock the socks off your employees by scheduling dynamic speakers to discuss a variety of health topics. Most communities boast many health and fitness professionals who are usually willing to give lectures at a minimal cost. To enlist people who can deliver focused and compelling presentations, contact health agencies such as hospitals, United Way, Blue Cross and Blue Shield, American Diabetes Association, state and county health departments, or agriculture extension services.

DEMONSTRATIONS

Sporting good stores usually jump at the chance to show the latest in sports shoes, clothing, and athletic gear. Invite them to present a ''Dress for Fitness'' fashion show. Who knows? Brand new jogging outfits may be just the ticket to motivate those workers who keep saying they'll begin exercising TOMORROW.

For demonstrations on breast self-examination, contact the American Cancer Society.

TESTIMONIALS

You can't find a more enthusiastic group than local community leaders and celebrities who have quit smoking, lost weight, or successfully adopted healthier life-style habits. Tap these folks for inspirational talks guaranteed to fire up employees about wellness.

WELLNESS BULLETIN BOARD

Opportunity doesn't have to knock when you've posted wellness material on a bulletin board that is highly visible to employees. Make sure that you update displays regularly.

HEALTH MAGAZINES AND NEWSLETTERS

Your employees will be treated to a bonanza of information if you subscribe to health journals and periodicals and circulate them or make them available in the break room or resource library. If your budget permits, indulge your workers and have publications sent by the company to their homes where they will have more leisure time for reading.

BLOOD PRESSURE KITS

Employees can learn to monitor their own cardiovascular health when you purchase easy-to-read blood pressure kits and make them readily available for use.

WELLNESS LOGO

Discover hidden employee talents and sponsor a logo contest. Use the wellness logo on everything involved with your health promotion program: awards, posters, stationery, and newsletter articles.

WELLNESS CALENDAR

Have planning calendars printed with daily health tips and monthly reminders for health checks. Employees will wonder how they ever got along without them.

FILMS

Everyone likes a good movie and there are lots of films available from health organizations. Films needn't always be strictly educational. A feature movie about an olympic athlete or a snorkeling trip in Mexico may inspire employees to get moving themselves.

WELCOME TO GOOD HEALTH!

HEALTH FAIRS

What do you have if you provide activities that draw attention to wellness, disease detection, disease prevention, and local health resources? A ready-made health fair.

You don't have to be an expert to dispense information on health topics, and that is what's so inviting about a health fair. Voluntary agencies for heart, cancer, diabetes, arthritis, Alzheimer's disease, and other chronic illnesses are usually very pleased to participate in health fairs. Agencies will:
- operate exhibits and booths
- provide disease screening and assessments
- give appropriate follow-ups for participants who need medical attention, further information, or education.

Health Fair Activities

You can assemble a treasure trove of resources for health fair goers if you explore a variety of creative ways to dispense information. Check ☑ the following methods that you could fit into your health fair:
- [ ] films
- [ ] lectures
- [ ] exhibits
- [ ] exercises
- [ ] pamphlets
- [ ] health games
- [ ] one act plays
- [ ] demonstrations
- [ ] screening tests
- [ ] learning centers

The most effective health fair exhibits are the ones that are continuously staffed and actively involve participants.

Educational Themes

Ideas for health fair exhibits are endless. Check ☑ the ones suitable for you and mastermind a few of your own.

- ☐ eye care
- ☐ first aid
- ☐ living habits
- ☐ mental health
- ☐ weight control
- ☐ healthy eating
- ☐ workplace health
- ☐ health insurance
- ☐ disease reduction
- ☐ stress management
- ☐ smoking cessation
- ☐ anatomy/physiology
- ☐ environmental health
- ☐ fitness and exercise
- ☐ alcohol and drug abuse

Add your own ideas: _____

_____

_____

Imagination At Work

On a warm day at a health fair in rural Ohio, a local hospital with limited funds sponsored a stand where they served a low-calorie health drink: cold water. Expenses were minimal since the cups were purchased at discount, yet the hospital got its health message across to folks who were attracted to a cool drink of water.

Health and Safety Agencies

You can rest assured that health fair participants are going to have access to the latest concepts in health and safety when they take advantage of the opportunities in a well-planned health fair.

Be sure to contact the health and safety agencies in your community to provide these "show and tell" good health concepts at the health fair.

"Mr. Yuk"—poison control center

911 demonstration—police department

Fire safety and "Pluggy"—fire department

Organ donation presentation—American Red Cross

Dental care/brushing techniques—dental association

Pulmonary function tests—American Lung Association

CPR demonstrations with "Annies"—American Red Cross

Babysitting safety tips—police and safety department

Self-esteem assessments—mental health/counseling clinic

Stress tab demonstrations—mental health clinic, hospital

Seat belt use—highway patrol, safety or police department

Safe cooking demonstrations—cooking school, adult education

Computerized alcohol assessments—Mothers Against Drunk Drivers

Body fat measurements—health department, hospital, medical center

Disability awareness (crutches, walkers, braces, wheelchairs)—rehabilitation center, hospital, nursing home

Screenings

You'll need a qualified team of health professionals and nonprofessionals to supervise the five basic health screenings.
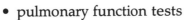
- vision
- blood pressure
- blood chemistry
- height and weight
- health checks (individual health assessment and goal setting)

Additional Screenings

Other special tests you may want to schedule in a health fair include:
- pap tests
- hearing tests
- glaucoma tests
- body fat tests
- foot screenings
- flexibility tests
- breast examinations
- pulmonary function tests

SECTION 5

MOVING ON—
PROGRAM
EVALUATION

PROGRAM EVALUATION

Evaluating a wellness program is a vital part of the program and can be just as exciting as program development. Evaluation can't be a last minute afterthought. The key to effective evaluation: develop the evaluation format while you're planning the program.

An evaluation need not be expensive, extensive, or conducted by experts. Each company needs to determine if it wants a formalized evaluation process, and if it does, what information it wants.

Evaluation of wellness programs is a relatively new field and there is disagreement about what to measure and how. Companies can start with simple evaluations and proceed to more complex evaluations as their programs expand. An evaluation can be as simple as randomly asking employees if they participated and, if so, what they got out of the health program.

Evaluations are conducted to see if goals have been met and if funds have been used efficiently. Evaluations also:

- chart the success of the program
- provide feedback for better budgeting
- provide companies and participants with progress and incentives
- provide the opportunity to review program content and the effectiveness of presentors

WHY EVALUATE?

It will help you decide on the kind of evaluation you need if you identify what you want to know. Check ☑ the following evaluation objectives:

Our company needs an evaluation to:

- ☐ determine the cost of the program
- ☐ determine which programs are the most effective
- ☐ determine which programs are the least effective
- ☐ determine if the program has met its goals
- ☐ justify past or future expenses
- ☐ justify program expansion
- ☐ gain greater control of the program
- ☐ contribute to the pool of health promotion information

EVALUATION PROCEDURE

The more boxes you have checked, the more information you need to complete your evaluation. Now, check off each step as you complete the evaluation process.

- ☐ Set measurable goals and objectives
- ☐ Decide the evaluation information needed by the company and employees
- ☐ Resolve how the data will be collected
- ☐ Determine who will analyze the data
- ☐ Decide when to conduct the evaluation
- ☐ Develop surveys and record-keeping tools
- ☐ Report on the evaluation findings

Easy, wasn't it? Just remember that nothing is impossible...until it is sent to a committee.

EXPANSION

There's no time like the present to expand your activities once wellness has been accepted among your employees. Infinite possibilities present themselves when you open the program to others.

How to Expand

Expansion can be accomplished in one of two ways.

1. Welcome family, retirees, and community members to selected activities that you are already planning for workers. Remember that since employees come first, available space is a major consideration. You won't want to open your programs to additional people unless there's room for all the employees who want to participate.
2. Besides regular wellness programming, plan specific activities and events for employees, families, and others. Offer family life seminars after work and feature such informative topics as dual careers, child discipline, money management, adolescent behavior, single parenting, and family communication.

Armco Corporation and St. Joseph Hospital are good examples of programs that work well.

Armco Corporation

The mailman plays a significant role in Armco Corporation's Safety for the Family Program that is operated in Middletown, Ohio. Each month employees receive a four-page mailing describing home, recreation, transportation, and public off-the-job hazards and preventive practices.

The company gives employees portfolios to store the safety tips that are mailed to them. Appointment calendars are also provided to remind employees of the monthly tips. On-the-job training is offered so employees can become their families' off-the-job safety leaders. Armco gets data from their employees and makes comparisons of accident rates before and after safety interventions.

St. Joseph Hospital

In Mitchell, South Dakota, St. Joseph Hospital's worksite wellness program was so successful in decreasing sick leave usage—saving $25,000 and decreasing hours lost by 3035—that they decided to expand their leadership role by extending health promotion activities to the community. The hospital sponsors annual health fairs, promotes nationally known conferences, performs screenings, and prescribes specific exercises to thousands of people in the community. The hospital also launched an aggressive marketing campaign that encourages area businesses to develop their own health promotion programs.

There's a wealth of activities that a company can sponsor to involve their community in wellness. You don't have to spend a lot of money to get effective public relations results. Watch these programs go to work for you:
- fun run
- health fairs
- fitness trail
- wellness walk
- tennis, racquetball, wallyball tournaments

WELLNESS COUNCILS

Your program can get a Herculean boost if a wellness council or health coalition is operating in your community. Health promotion councils may differ in approach, but all are designed to help promote wellness at the worksite. Read on to discover the ABCs of coalitions and councils.

Whys and Wherefores

A. Companies in Nebraska are in luck, because they can join the Wellness Council of the Midlands. This council, and others like it across the country, provide technical assistance to member businesses that request help with planning, implementing, or evaluating wellness programs. Other U.S. groups offer educational programs or provide information services such as newsletters, other printed materials, audiovisuals, and resource directories.
B. A large number of coalitions sponsor conferences on wellness that feature national experts on health topics. The Minnesota Coalition on Health is a sterling example of a coalition that is addressing the rapidly rising costs of health care. You can bet that several hundred business and labor leaders paid close attention when the Minnesota Coalition sponsored a seminar about the surprisingly low costs of Canada's government-financed health care system.
C. When small businesses can't individually afford the cost of a particular health promotion program, councils and coalitions can bring the businesses together to share the costs.

Contact the ODPHP Health Information Center or the Wellness Councils of America to locate coalitions or councils in your area. You will find their addresses listed in the resource section of this book.

SIXTEEN WAYS TO JAZZ UP A TIRED PROGRAM

If your wellness program is three or four years old and its novelty has worn off, chances are that you need to identify ideas that will renew interest in your efforts. The following questions will help you to evaluate areas that can spark program planning.

YES   **NO**

☐   ☐   **1.** Have you promoted wellness with employee success stories?

Allow workers to talk or write about significant health behavior changes (weight loss, smoking cessation, etc.) This encourages other employees to get into the act. Schedule a noontime seminar where employees can share their experiences, or encourage workers to write about health success stories in the company newsletter.

☐   ☐   **2.** Have you tried a staff exchange program?

Plan to share employee talent by arranging a short exchange with workers in other companies who are responsible for health programs and presentations.

☐   ☐   **3.** Do you work in conjunction with other existing activities in your company?

Offer to check blood pressures at staff meetings, or set up pulmonary function tests at the summer picnic.

☐   ☐   **4.** Have you closed down the program for a few months?

A short respite allows staff and participants to re-energize for a new "wellness season."

YES	NO
☐	☐

5. Do you use volunteers from outside the company?

Volunteers can do wonders to perk up a program and help spread the word about your wellness effort. Recruit retired people or college students to help plan and implement health activities.

☐	☐

6. Do you use local celebrities to give testimonials on the positive health changes they have made?

Sports and political figures and area radio and television personalities are usually pleased to share their successful experiences.

☐	☐

7. Have you tried a new look?

Take a new direction with a different logo, theme, or even a new name to give your wellness program a lift.

☐	☐

8. Do you have a health promotion advisory committee with rotating members?

A continuous flow of new members provides fresh ideas.

☐	☐

9. Are awards to participants presented quarterly or annually?

Recognition of special achievement helps motivate employees who are participating in the programs and those procrastinating about doing so.

☐	☐

10. Have you changed the emphasis of your program lately?

If your direction has been physical fitness, enhance the program by adding mental fitness or spiritual program choices.

SIXTEEN WAYS TO JAZZ UP A TIRED PROGRAM (Continued)

YES	NO		
☐	☐	**11.**	Do you emphasize socialization and team spirit?
			Promote activities that bring employees together to have fun. Have a picnic with a wellness walk or a softball game.
☐	☐	**12.**	Have you taken programs to different locations in your facility?
			Try a program in the dining area and supply a nutritional snack. If programs are usually offered in the auditorium, schedule them in decentralized locations. Or, if it's a nice day, have everyone sit outside.
☐	☐	**13.**	Have you explored different employee groups that would benefit from health promotion programs?
			Women's issues are a good place to begin. Concerns of working mothers, pregnancy issues, or breast self-examination classes will pique the interest of many women.
☐	☐	**14.**	Do you have programs featuring topics that are receiving television coverage or attention in popular magazines?
			The latest medical breakthroughs and research findings about vitamins or medicines are always popular subjects.
☐	☐	**15.**	Is management actively committed to a wellness program?
			Invite a senior manager to take part in a volleyball game or attend a class in defensive driving.
☐	☐	**16.**	Are your incentives irresistible?
			Why not have a drawing each month (or each quarter) for program participants to receive a paid ''health day'' off?

LET'S GET GOING!

If you are still asking why your company should be involved in employee wellness, the answer is, "you already are." Each year your company stays in business, you can expect to pay more for poor employee health.

Why not take the challenge and try some of the health promotion ideas suggested in this book? Be prepared for quick, indirect results in the form of improved attitude and morale. Decreased costs and increased productivity won't happen overnight and can take as long as three to four years while the health interventions begin to take effect. But the pay-off in improved employee health and dollars will come.

In the meantime, remember to make the program fun, flexible, and interactive. And give it the high visibility it deserves to make it successful.

Wellness never grows old. Caring for oneself mentally and physically is a lifelong experience. You can be certain that once you have created an opportunity for your employees to learn about wellness, their healthy smiles will be worth their weight in gold.

SECTION 6

RESOURCES

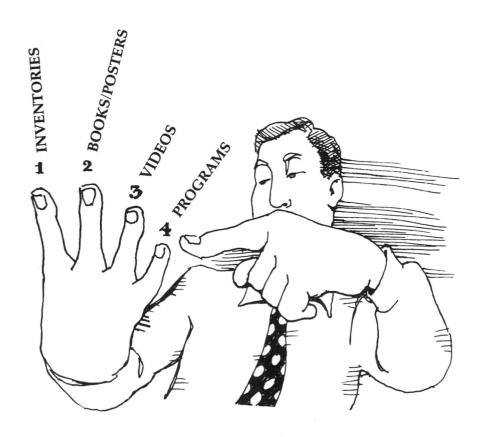

RESOURCES

INVENTORIES

Healthstyle: A Self-Test
ODPHP National Health Information Center
P.O. Box 1133
Washington, D.C. 20013-1133

Order Number H0012. $1 handling fee.

Health Protection Plan
Preventive Medicine Institute/Strang Clinic
55 East 34th Street
New York, N.Y. 10016

Free. Risk factors for 8 kinds of cancer, plus heart disease and stroke.

APPRAISALS

Health Risk Appraisal
Centers for Disease Control
Center for Health Promotion and Education
Program Services and Development Branch
1600 Clifton Road
Atlanta, Georgia 30333

NUTRITION

Food and Nutrition Information Center
National Agricultural Library
Room 304
Bellsville, Maryland 20705

Consumer Information Center
Pueblo, Colorado 81009

American Dietetic Association
430 North Michigan Avenue
Chicago, Illinois 60611
(or your local association)

HYPERTENSION

American Heart Association
7320 Greenville Avenue
Dallas, Texas 75231
(or your local chapter)

National High Blood Pressure Education Program Information Center
4733 Bethesda Avenue
Room 530
Bethesda, Maryland 20814

STRESS MANAGEMENT

National Clearinghouse for Mental Health Information
5600 Fishers Lane
Rockville, Maryland 20857

National Mental Health Association
1800 North Kent Street
Arlington, Virginia 22209

FITNESS AND EXERCISE

President's Council on Physical Fitness and Sports
450 5th Street, N.W.
Suite 7103
Washington, D.C. 20001

SMOKING CESSATION

American Lung Association
1740 Broadway
New York, New York 10019

Office of Cancer Communications
National Cancer Institute
9000 Rockville Pike
Bethesda, Maryland 20205

RESOURCES (Continued)

SMOKING CESSATION (Con't)

Office of Smoking and Health
Technical Information Center, Park Building
5600 Fishers Lane
Rockville, Maryland 20857

ALCOHOL AND DRUG PREVENTION

National Clearinghouse for Alcohol and Drug Information
P.O. Box 2345
Rockville, Maryland 20852

Alcoholics Anonymous
General Services Office (6th floor)
468 Park Avenue South
New York, New York 10016
(or your local chapter)

WEIGHT CONTROL

Weight Watchers International, Inc.
800 Community Drive
Manhassett, New York 11030
(or your local chapter)

American Dietetic Association
430 North Michigan Avenue
Chicago, Illinois 60611

SAFETY AND ACCIDENT PREVENTION

National Safety Council
444 North Michigan Avenue
Chicago, Illinois 60611

SAFETY AND ACCIDENT PREVENTION (Con't)

Clearinghouse for Occupational Safety and Health Information
4676 Columbia Parkway
Cincinnati, Ohio 45226

Your local Red Cross teaches first-aid and CPR for a minimal fee.

EMPLOYEE ASSISTANCE PROGRAMS

American Hospital Association
Center for Health Promotion
840 North Lake Shore Drive
Chicago, Illinois 60611

National Institute on Drug Abuse
1-800-843-4971 (Hotline to help establish or modify employee assistance programs)

WELLNESS COALITIONS AND COUNCILS

ODPHP National Health Information Center
P.O. Box 1133
Washington, D.C. 20013-1133

Wellness Councils of America
Historic Library Plaza
1823 Harney Street
Suite 201
Omaha, Nebraska 68102

GENERAL WELLNESS PROGRAM INFORMATION

ODPHP National Health Information Center
P.O. Box 1133
Washington, D.C. 20013-1133

Centers for Disease Control
Center for Health Promotion and Education
Atlanta, Georgia 30333

NOTES

FOR OTHER FIFTY-MINUTE SELF-STUDY BOOKS
SEE THE BACK OF THIS BOOK.

ABOUT THE FIFTY-MINUTE SERIES

We hope you enjoyed this book and found it valuable. If so, we have good news for you. This title is part of the best selling *FIFTY-MINUTE Series* of books. All other books are similar in size and identical in price. Several books are supported with a training video. These are identified by the symbol **Ⓥ** next to the title.

Since the first *FIFTY-MINUTE* book appeared in 1986, more than five million copies have been sold worldwide. Each book was developed with the reader in mind. The result is a concise, high quality module written in a positive, readable self-study format.

FIFTY-MINUTE Books and Videos are available from your distributor or from Crisp Publications, Inc., 95 First Street, Los Altos, CA 94022. A free current catalog is available on request.

The complete list of *FIFTY-MINUTE Series* Books and Videos are listed on the following pages and organized by general subject area.

MANAGEMENT TRAINING (Cont.)

PERSONNEL/HUMAN RESOURCES

COMMUNICATIONS

CUSTOMER SERVICE/SALES TRAINING (CONT.)

SMALL BUSINESS/FINANCIAL PLANNING

ADULT LITERACY/BASIC LEARNING

CAREER BUILDING

To order books/videos from the FIFTY-MINUTE Series, please:

1. **CONTACT YOUR DISTRIBUTOR**

   or

2. **Write to Crisp Publications, Inc.**
   95 First Street   (415) 949-4888 - phone
   Los Altos, CA 94022   (415) 949-1610 - FAX